Psychology

of

Serial Killers

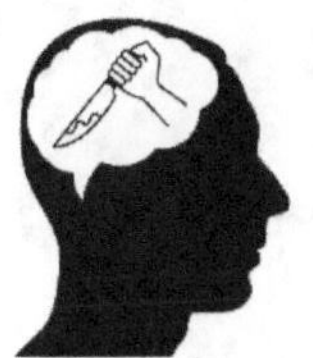

A Concise Guide with Jaw-Dropping Content.

By

Rio Riley

Table of Contents

Psychology of Serial Killers

A serial killer is a person who performs a series of crimes at least three murders over some time of more than a month, with the killings interspersed by considerable periods. Serial homicides must be unique from one another and virtually usually driven by some kind of psychological high or pleasure for the perpetrator to be considered a serial killer. As a result of their lack of empathy and guilt, as well as their predisposition to become egocentric individuals, some serial killers are psychopaths. A "mask of normalcy" is one of the most popular disguises worn by serial killers to hide their true psychopath tendencies. Even though serial killers are classified as a different category, there are conceptual parallels between them and other types of mass murderers. For example, the difference between serial murderers and spree killers has sparked some controversy among experts.

When a person has murdered three or more individuals who were previously unknown to him or her, serial murder is the rarest kind of homicide, with a 'cooling-off time between each murder. As well-known as serial murderers are in our day and age, their roots may be traced back to ancient Rome.

It has been established by criminologists that there are two distinct types of serial murder: traditional serial murder (often including stalking and sexual motives) and spree serial murder (typically fueled by thrill-seeking). For the most part, serial killings are not motivated by profit, unlike political assassinations and terrorist acts or professional murder performed by the criminal community. There is a general belief that serial killers are motivated by a sexual urge or even by a desire to have fun. Many murders are carried out to give the killers a sense of control over their victims, which may or may not be sexual. There have been several different groups of people that have been targeted by the gangs. Popular culture has given a lot of attention to serial killers, in part because of the way they are portrayed as personifications of evil.

Many people are baffled as to why serial murderers engage in such heinous acts. Most criminologists agree that serial murderers' conduct is a direct result of early trauma. The "Homicide Triad," which describes the characteristics of a serial murderer as a youngster, is the most important component in their growth. A serial killer's "Homicide Triad," which involves bed-wetting, arson, and animal cruelty as a youngster, is one of the most typical characteristics. As a result, this term is widely recognized by both police and academics, making it a helpful framework. The problem, however, is that it restricts the investigation of serial killings since it fails to integrate many of the well-known aspects of serial murders. their horrible actions, serial killers have always attracted the general public because they represent the extremities to which mental illness may lead a person. The lives of serial murderers are analyzed to the tiniest detail in the name of psychological insight to discover what circumstances contribute to forming a 'monster'. Criminals who commit many killings in a short period are said to be engaging in serial murder, according to the Crime Classification Manual.

As opposed to the stereotypical, isolated, and psychotic serial killer, we've chosen to examine the disturbingly familiar reality of today's mass murderer. Institutional frameworks, incentives, and opportunity structures for studying such behaviors have emerged as a result of the mass media's rise, anonymity, star culture, and specific cultural frameworks of denunciation. It is because of this larger social context that concentrating solely on the etiology and offenders' histories overlooks this more complicated understanding of serial killing.

Serial murderers are influenced by a wide range of media outlets, as well as their inclination to target victims from certain socioeconomic backgrounds. These (and other) characteristics may provide light on the larger social and historical circumstances in which such actions take place. Even though serial killings are statistically uncommon, they are a common cultural phenomenon that is best comprehended by the great majority of people as a media event. Film, television, literature, real crime, and video games all include serial murderers as a central theme. It is a peculiarity of modernity that many people are aware of the dynamics of serial killing and the lives of especially infamous criminals thanks to this worldwide mass media. However, the media's role in the serial killing is not always clear-cut. The mass media has made the term "serial killer" a dominant cultural category by broadly disseminating information about particular serial murderers. While in ancient someone could be a serial murderer, now anybody can be one. The media's widespread use of the term "serial killer" makes the specifics of this type of behavior susceptible to imitation. This does not, however, rule out the idea that more sophisticated "media effect" situations act as structural preconditions for such crimes as serial murders.

Relationships between individuals have experienced significant changes as a consequence of the anonymity that comes with mega-

unparalleled urbanization. In pre-modern times, everyone in the neighborhood knew each other's identities and family histories, therefore there were no privacy concerns. It was because of this that the few individuals who were able to interact with the outside world became the topic of rumor and suspicion. If you're a modern-day citizen, hundreds of individuals are likely to pass you as you go to work every day. Individuals found themselves in a sea of strangers as a consequence of widespread migration to metropolitan areas and the advent of capitalism. Because serial murderers are well-known for preying on the helpless and defenseless, this development prepared the way for an increase in the frequency and severity of serial murders When compared to most homicide cases, when the perpetrator and victim had a previous connection, these murders are unique. Since serial murder is so easy to do in today's densely populated cities, it has grown increasingly commonplace.

Classic serial murder, which typically includes stalking and is often driven by a desire for sexual gratification, is distinct from spree serial murder, which is more likely to be motivated by thrill-seeking. For-profit is not an evident logical reason in most serial killings, which separates them from political assassinations and terrorism and gangster-committed professional murders. People presume that those who commit serial killings do it for reasons such as sexual compulsion or even amusement. Murders may experience a sense of power over their victims, which may or may not be sexual, as a result of their actions. Migrant women, child prostitutes, and vagrants are among the most common targets. In part, because they are seen as personifications of evil, serial killers have garnered a great deal of media attention.

In the last three decades, law enforcement, physicians, and academics. Even though these definitions have a lot in common, they vary on several key points, such as the number of killings, the motives, and the time frame in which the crimes were committed. Attendees of the Serial Murder Symposium evaluated these disparities to come up with a single definition for serial killing. Serial murder had previously been defined as a certain number of killings, ranging from two to 10. Serial murder was separated from other types of homicides by this quantitative criterion (i.e. single, double, or triple murder).

In most cases, the time elapsed between the killings was also needed under the definitions. Mass murders and serial killings may be distinguished only by such interruptions in time. Separate occasions, cooling-off periods, and emotional cooling-off phases were all used to characterize the time between killings in serial homicide.

Typically, mass murder was defined as a series of four or more murders happening at the same time, with no discernible time interval between the killings. In most cases, a single location served as the setting for a series of simultaneous murders by a single assailant.

Legislation attempting to define serial murder has been introduced at least once. A definition of serial murders is included in this legislation:

"Serial murder is defined in the United States as a sequence of three or more murders, one of which is articulated by a single offender or culprits".

The federal law defines serial murder, but its use is restricted. This definition's goal was to define criteria for when the FBI may help local authorities investigating suspected serial killings. A general definition of serial murder was not the intention.

The benefits and drawbacks of the many definitions proposed at the Symposium were hotly debated. Attendees agreed on the need for a concise but comprehensive description that would be useful to law enforcement officials.

The discussion revolved over how many killings were required to be classified as serial murder in this case. As a result, many academics and researchers sought to define a certain number of killings to set criteria for their investigations of serial murderers. Law enforcement may devote more resources to a possible serial murder investigation if the criteria allowed for fewer victims than originally intended.

Attendees thought that the inclusion of motive in a broad definition was unnecessary since it would make the definition too complicated

We had a lively discussion on the issue of spree murder during our panel discussion. As a rule, a spree killer is someone who kills two or more people at the same time without taking a pause interval in between. According to this definition, a spree killing differs from a serial killing in that there is no cooling-off period. The dispute revolved around the concept of a "cooling-off period" and its definition. Because of the ambiguity surrounding this concept, the majority of participants suggested that the term "spree murder" be dropped. For law enforcement reasons, this categorization is of no utility at all.

Psychology Behind The Serial Killers

People become serial killers for several reasons. After committing three or more murders, these are the people who have cooled off emotionally between each. Because serial murderers lack basic human emotions like empathy, remorse, or regret, they are among the scariest psychopaths. Caucasian male serial killers are more likely to target white victims. More than 84% of serial killers are white, 90% of the victims are male, and 89% of the victims are likewise white. Most serial killers are Lust Murderers, who kill to fulfill their sexual appetites. Torturing a victim gives a serial killer more and greater satisfaction with each act.

When it comes to serial killers, their origins may be traced to the Roman Empire. Five prostitutes were murdered by Jack the Ripper in

London in 1888, and he has long been regarded as the first modern serial killer. When serial killing became a major concern, law enforcement tried to classify it as a new kind of crime. The United States is home to the great majority of the world's serial killers. Seventy-six percent of the world's serial killers reside in the United States. It's not clear why serial killers display such chaotic behavior despite a surge in the number of murders. Many are confused by the motives of serial killers. Serial killers' people behavior is a direct outcome of childhood trauma, according to most criminologists. The "Homicide Triad," which characterizes the qualities of a serial killer as a youth, is the most crucial factor in their development… Another prevalent trait of an early-life serial murderer is the "Homicide Triad," which includes incidents of bed-wetting, fire, and animal abuse.

The three behaviors are:

- setting fires,
- wetting the bed,
- and being cruel.

For me, it's a popular belief that serial murderers are arsonists because they have a "fascination owing to their desire for dramatic damage". He believes that as serial killers become older, their need for destruction grows and they resort to murder as a means of satiating that desire. There are similar threads among serial murderers, such as sadistic activities, bed-wetting, and fire-starting, that support the hypothesis that early events influence psychopathic conduct. When it comes to the "Homicide Triad," sadistic daydreaming is a typical trait among serial killers. Sadistic fantasizing was often an issue for serial murderers as youngsters. Daydreams involving sex and violence were the norm. "Future serial murderers develop sexual fantasies as toddlers to assist regulate their anxiety and it is a means to release hatred and violence towards others When a youngster is being abused, he or she may turn to sexual fantasies as a way to cope. As youngsters, their daydreams give them the power to govern their own lives, the lives of others, and the course of history. In addition, they indulge in sexual fantasies to make up for the lack of affection they had in their lives. Serial murderers' childhood fantasies often include things like kicking a dog to get it to listen to them, beating them, and even murdering their parents. For the majority of serial murderers, childhood sadistic fantasizing is a primary factor in their development.

The majority of serial murderers have been found to have had a problem with excessive day deeming as youngsters. As youngsters, they would fantasize about being cruel, and as adults, they would put those dreams into action. When Ted Bundy was three, he started carrying knives around with him because he had the idea of controlling people with them. When he was older, he used knives on at least fifty women as a replacement for his mother, whom he fantasized about murdering multiple times but was unable to carry through. Even while cruel daydreams as a youngster might lead to serial killer behavior, maltreatment as a child is the greatest common denominator of serial murderers.

As a youngster, most serial murderers have been subjected to a variety of physical and emotional abuse. Adolescents who have been subjected to sexual, psychological, or physical abuse as children tend to hold grudges toward those who have not treated them well in the past. Of all serial murderers, more than a third (35%) were sexually abused as youngsters. Until he was eighteen

The early experiences of serial murderers are strongly linked to their growth as a killer. The "Homicide Triads," such as teenage bed-wetting, arson, or cruel behavior, are common characteristics among serial murderers. This supports the hypothesis that serial murderers' early circumstances directly influence their psychopathic conduct. Psychiatrists and other role models should be on the lookout for these signs in their children and assist them to get them. There should be an investigation of the underlying reasons for a person's actions when they commit crimes as children. Youngsters can escape confronting the harsh realities of life by daydreaming about sexual or violent fantasies. To prevent the youngster from daydreaming, family members, teachers, and friends should be more active in the child's life. Getting more engaged in the kid's life can help the parents recognize that their child has a mental health issue and seek care before it gets any worse, thereby preventing future harm. A youngster who is abused as a child develops a hatred for others as a result of the trauma. Serial murderers are motivated to exact retribution on the people who caused them so much suffering as children, because of the psychological, physical, and sexual abuse they endured. As long as others in the community take action and report child abuse rather than not doing so, the hate formed from the abuse may end and the kid may have a chance to have an otherwise normal life.

Generally speaking, serial murderers' childhoods provide a glimpse into what makes them tick. Many hypotheses and techniques exist as to why serial murderers commit their crimes. The majority of these hypotheses are based on notions of child abuse, although they use a variety of developmental and psychological methods to solve the mystery of serial killings as their starting point. Science, as we all know, is a process of constant experimentation, thus nothing on these pages should be considered gospel.

The themes of sexual tension, parental over-protection, or outright rejection, are used by some to explain serial murder. Other views claim that the murderer's childhood guilt stops him from having sex with his victim to the extent that he has to "forgive" him. , who was a serial murderer, it is more pleasant to have sexual relations with a dead person since the body cannot reject him, is never disloyal, and has no sexual expectations. In addition, the serial killer may be able to overcome emotions of inadequacy and inferiority through killing. To remind the serial killer of his "creation," he or she may take the victim's trophies or document the action in a book, for example.

Many serial murderers have also spoken of their hate for a key female. One theory is that mutilations are the murderers' way of trying to go back inside the mother's body and explore it again. In addition, serial murderers have a history dating back to their youth. There must be some connection between the murderers' animosity against their mother and the maltreatment they suffered as children. Before reaching harmful levels, he argued that forceful energy build-up should be frequently dissipated. If it were not released, it may lead to actions like serial murders. However, many feel that such anger may be expressed without resorting to violence and that this idea cannot be used to explain serial killings.

This is what I discussed at the beginning of this work, the development method. To understand why these creatures, exist, I've been repeating this hypothesis over and over again. The childhood symptoms are examined in more detail in this method. Arson, animal cruelty, and bedwetting are all discussed from this angle. Some argue that children's habit of wetting the bed is an act of defiance against their parents. An animal's torture is another sort of revolt against the idea of maintaining pets as treasured companions. Children who have been subjected to physical abuse as children are more likely to become serial murderers. There is a loss of self-worth, a lack of social skills, a sense of powerlessness, an inability to make choices, and an inability to plan one's future as a result of this abuse. People who have been sexually abused tend to retreat into their imaginations. People who are being mistreated may assume that the abuse is occurring to someone else to save themselves from going insane. An abuse victim's dream world might become reality, and this is when the homicides may begin to take place.

Serial killers' personalities are a hot-button issue that has sparked a lot of debate. Other personality qualities have been linked to serial killer activity, including psychopathic personality disorder. Serial murderers have impulsiveness, little empathy, and poor social skills. Serial murderers with poor self-esteem are more likely to display antisocial conduct and high sensitivity to criticism. Average to high intellect may help a serial murderer evade police arrest and discover if intelligence can be linked to personality. Criminals with such high IQs may explain why it takes so long for authorities to apprehend a serial killer. It has long been debated whether serial murderers' personalities have a factor in their crimes. The only way to know for sure if a serial killer has committed his or her crimes is to conduct the necessary tests on him or her. In criminal psychology, law enforcement agencies, and the general public have long sought to understand what drives serial murderers to carry out their heinous deeds of violence. Most "normal" people would never consider committing such heinous acts of violence, thus it's unclear whether or not serial killers suffer from a mental illness that leads them to lose touch with reality.

Although there have been a few instances in which serial killers are legally insane, this is not the norm. Most serial murderers have an antisocial personality traits: they lack empathy, show no sign of regret, disregard the rule of law and society in general, and have a strong desire to exact retribution on those who have wronged them or on society as a whole by committing horrifying crimes.

Addiction treatment is the last strategy I'll discuss. There are fascinating facets to the approach's name, which is self-explanatory. Alcoholics, on the other hand, have the same mentality. Similarly, to the notion of frustration/aggression, the individual feels uneasy in-between offenses and is relieved of that unease after a kill is achieved. The murderers' need for blood grows as time passes between kills. When a kill is made, they experience a sense of peace (this calmness could give the person a feeling of at ease and the ability to sleep). There is a possibility that the serial killer is hooked on his bizarre behavior in the same way that pornography and sex addicts are. They may have killed so many people because of their addiction.

Serial killers, there should be some warning signs before it reaches the point of murder. There are many tiers of society in today's culture, and not everyone pays special attention to their relationships with close relatives and friends. The child's violent conduct may be prevented if the potential murderer received therapy to help them recover from their maltreatment. Many lives might be spared if society got engaged and ensured that every kid was loved and cared for. According to this research, serial murderers are formed as youngsters due to the abuse they suffer. An individual's road to becoming the most horrifying of psychopaths—the Serial Killer—is paved with early childhood trauma.

Those who commit serial murders are motivated by a deep-seated desire to cause pain and suffering to others. This apparent discrepancy in emotional responses still needs a neurobiological explanation. As a society, we cannot ignore the role of social pressures in shaping these opposing impulses. Somehow, it seems as though serial killers have learned to see their victims as nothing more than a jumble of unrelated parts. Although it might explain why some murderers have sex with their victims or even utilize their bodies for utilitarian or aesthetic reasons, it does not solve the issue of why they seem to be so impelled to harm and kill their victims. The fear of being rejected is common among serial killers, which might explain the latter phenomenon. One or both parents' abandonment or maltreatment as children is a common cause for fear of being rejected today. Because of their paranoia, serial killers may be tempted to murder anybody or anything they find appealing... There is a risk in believing they may prevent being abandoned, humiliated, or otherwise wounded in infancy by removing the person they want.

Additionally, serial murderers tend to lack a feeling of societal responsibility. Children are taught to differentiate good from wrong via the influence of their parents and other adults they interact with throughout their lives. Despite this, serial murderers appear to believe that they are free from the most significant societal penalty of all—the prohibition against murdering another person. As an example, you don't have to. It's beyond your abilities. I'm a completely different kind of person than you are. It is no good or bad in me.

For some people who have been tortured or traumatized early in life, it isn't clear why they subsequently become serial murderers. By learning more about their mental and neurological makeup, we may be able to prevent future tragedies like this from occurring.

Psychopathology Of Serial Killers

To, being labeled with psychopath means a man is a depraved, selfish psychopath who takes advantage of others by robbing them of their possessions and liberties. Psychopaths have no respect for the feelings or rights of others, and they act without hesitation or regret. To describe someone whose psychopath is a result of factors such as their genetic makeup, social environment, and early life experiences, we would use the term "psychopath." As with psychopaths, sociopaths exhibit the same behavior and personality traits. Sociopaths, on the other hand, are the glaring exception to this rule, since their upbringing and social environment are what caused their sickness in the first place. Serial killers tend to suffer from emotional and behavioral instability. Because the term "instability" has so many different connotations, it should be used cautiously. There should be no presumption that the average person has a fixed attitude or emotional-affective reaction in this situation since this would contradict the idea of continuous adaptation to changing environmental demands. To maintain a stable temperament, an individual must plan out the duration of his or her reactions, avoid excessive oscillations, and remain consistent in terms of both quantity and quality while responding appropriately to the stimuli that have triggered them. The killer's reactions to stimuli are inconsistent and unpredictable, as shown by the sudden changes in his look and the unjustified leaps from one extreme to the other.

Disobedience to social standards, as shown by their contempt for rules and regulations that define acceptable behavior, is another trait of serial killers The absence of organized educational and social forces is a constant source of struggle for these misfits. As a consequence, these families usually exhibit structural or functional flaws, such as the death, divorce, imprisonment, or desertion of a parent. Due to poor socio-economic and cultural levels and alcoholism, as well as criminal problems, a family may be structurally sound but lacking in the ability or willingness to properly educate a kid. Even if we overlook the reality that these families are inescapable, many prospective offenders may be detected. Because they believe that education is a self-sufficient process that does not necessitate parental involvement or oversight, wealthy and culturally affluent families should not be excluded from this discussion. Instead, they prefer to apply sporadic corrections and sanctions only when their children's behavior deviates from established norms. As a general rule, most people think that maladjustment is triggered when youngsters focus too much on the social standards of daily life, especially during their formative years. Serial killers who were known to have had sexual relations with a woman in their youth were, on the whole, dissatisfied with their romantic relationships. There is nothing of significance left for them. Serial killers have claimed to have been abused as children in some instances, most often by their mother or another parent or grandmother. They said that while they were drunk or drugged, they couldn't appreciate the intensity and savagery of their actions and had no legitimate explanation for their actions. There was a correlation between sobriety and homicide committed under the influence of intoxicants and psychotropic drugs, according to a study.

The number of murders committed by a serial killer tends to increase with time. They need to commit more murders to satisfy their antipathy to the act. As they got more reckless and careless in their pursuit, several serial killers were caught by accident. Criminals won't stop killing until they are caught and sentenced to life in prison. A sexually sadistic psychopath who develops into a serial killer cannot be rehabilitated.

Both criminal justice officials and academics have paid more attention to the link between psychopathy and serial murder in recent years. Serial murderers often exhibit a unique set of interpersonal, emotional, lifestyle, and antisocial characteristics and behaviors that are characteristic of psychopathy, according to the results of a recent FBI symposium on serial murder. Deception, manipulative, impulsive, stimulation-seeking behavior, a lack of empathy and guilt, a callous disdain for the rights of others and unethical and antisocial conduct are some of the features and behaviors that the FBI has identified as being associated with these people. The psychopath is defined by these characteristics, although they begin to appear in infancy. Serial murderers that are psychopathic are capable of deciphering right from wrong and are well-versed in the criminal justice system. They are aware, in particular, that murder is a crime against society's norms and laws. They are aware that they are bound by social norms, yet they choose to flout them to further their own narrow, self-centered goals.

Psychopathic assassins often conceal their identities in plain sight.

Due to the criminal justice system's definition of insanity, psychopathic serial murderers are seldom acquitted due to their mental state. However, contrary to common belief, psychopathic serial murderers are not insane in the clinical or legal senses, and so are not schizophrenics. When it comes to delusions and drug misuse, they aren't as common as they used to be (unless they also have a different mental condition such as psychosis). The counsel for a psychopathic serial murderer may use psychotic delusions as a defense in the criminal courts. Because psychotic delusions are not a feature of psychopathy, prosecutors are usually able to disprove these accusations.

Psychopathic serial murderers have a lack of empathy for their victims and a disrespect for their pain. They are seldom enraged by their victims. They're more prone to treat them with a chilly indifference. When a serial killer stalks and kills a victim, he or she generally goes into a trance and has a dissociative impact on their emotions.

SERIAL KILLERS IN THE LIGHT OF NEUROSCIENCES:

here is a mixture of disgust and fascination with serial killers—those who commit murders over and over again—in the general society. Modern psychology and neuroscience, on the other hand, may provide light on what could be going on in the minds of such people. The lack of empathy and seeming lack of remorse shown by serial murderers is a defining trait of their behavior. At the same time, many can entice prospective victims into their web of ruin by seeming to be likable on the surface. Serial murderers are said to have two minds: one reasonable self-capable of navigating the complexities of appropriate social conduct and even charming and seducing others, and a much more sinister self-capable of the most horrific and brutal atrocities against others.

Because DID is more often connected with victims of abuse than offenders, those who suffer from it develop many identities as a method of coping with the trauma they have endured. Many serial murderers have been the victims of abuse as children, yet they seem to be individuals who are aware of their actions rather than divided personalities. The dichotomy in the minds of such people is perhaps best exemplified by the US killer Ted Bundy, who was a "charming and handsome, successful individual [yet also] a sadist, necrophilia, rapist, and murderer with zero remorse who took pride in his ability to successfully kill and evade capture," according to the FBI.

There is a strong emotional drive in serial murderers that leads to a want to harm and kill others. Neurological explanations are still needed for this apparent mismatch in emotional reactions. Social effects are vital in the formation of such contradicting drives, however, and should not be ignored. Perhaps serial murderers can regard their victims as nothing more than an item to be mistreated, or even an assemblage of unrelated pieces. Even if this were the case, it still does not explain why certain murderers engage in sexual activity with the corpses of their victims or use them as decorative accents. Insecure serial murderers may be motivated to kill by a pathological dread of being rejected, a possible explanation for this phenomenon. When it comes to rejection anxiety, many individuals have a traumatic past in which they were abandoned and/or abused by a parent(s). A young assassin's fear of becoming a serial killer may lead them to kill everyone who catches their attention. Some may develop to believe that they would no longer be abandoned or humiliated as youngsters if they murder the person they desire.

Additionally, serial murderers tend to lack a feeling of societal responsibility. We develop the ability to tell right from wrong as children thanks to the guidance of our parents, siblings, teachers, and other adults in our lives. As a result of this, we are unable to engage in antisocial behavior. There is a pervasive belief among serial murderers, however, that they are immune from the most fundamental social rule: not killing another person. It's not something you're capable of. I have a different perspective than you do. When it comes down to it, I am neither good nor bad... "I don't believe in this so-called civilized society's hypocritical, moralistic doctrine."

At this moment, there is no recognized reason for those who have been mistreated or traumatized in the past to become serial murderers. For such catastrophes to be avoided, we must understand more about the psychological and neurological systems that underpin their acts.

Typical of serial murderers is their lack of compassion and empathy for the victims of their crimes, as well as their lack of sense of shame or remorse. While at the same time, virtually all of them can entice victims by seeming to be attractive on the surface. There are two possible explanations for why serial killers can successfully navigate the complexity of socially acceptable behavior and even seduce and charm, while their other self can perform the most heinous and heinous acts in which a person has more than two personalities in their mind that are unaware of one another. The evidence to back this claim, on the other hand, is scanty.

Due to their inability to feel the pain and sadness of others, serial killers are unable to sympathize with their victims. These findings were corroborated by brand-new imaging investigations of the brain. Findings from those research demonstrate that serial murderers have fewer connections between their amygdala (a portion of their brain that analyses negative stimuli and elevates their fear responses), as well as their prefrontal cortex (a region that handles rational thought) (which clarifies the responses that the amygdala creates).

As a result of the diminished connection between these areas, negative stimuli are not acknowledged and do not result in unpleasant feelings. Psychopaths' murderers may be able to explain why they don't feel any remorse for their actions or feel regret.

In addition, they are said to have an elevated emotional drive that makes them prone to violence or aggression. These kinds of emotional reactions aren't well understood, and more research is needed to shed light on them. Nevertheless, the societal impact should not be discounted as a contributor to the development of such drives. As a consequence, they've likely come to see their victims as nothing more than trash to be thrown away. This might explain why some of them opt to use the corpses of their victims as mementos or artifacts, or even engage in sexual relations with them.

There's also the possibility that many of them are insecure individuals driven to self-destruction by a deep-seated dread of being rejected. In most situations, the dread stems from parental abuse or abandonment. Meaning that they believe that destroying the person who has injured them, humiliated, or abandoned them in the past would prevent it from happening again.

ORGANIZED AND DISORGANIZED SERIAL KILLERS:

Disorganized and organized serial murderers are often discussed and used as examples of this dichotomous categorization system. In the scientific literature, there is just one small-scale, empirical test of this concept, and that research has several major flaws. If you're looking for 'offender profiles' to support police investigations and in certain murder prosecutions, this typology is sometimes used as the basis for the creation of a 'criminal profile' despite its apparent flaws. The organized/disorganized dichotomy's assumptions may be tested using data from the murder scene, which can be acquired from law enforcement. Components of the model may be examined at the crime scene for any underlying structure using well-established psychometric procedures. As a first step in evaluating this model, the crime sites of 100 killings committed by a hundred serial killers in the United States were examined for the presence of 39 serial killing traits.

25 first-degree killers and 11 people convicted of sexually assaulting or sexually abusing another person. The categorization method identified 24 organized and 12 disorganized killers in this group. Both the murder site and the backdrop of the two groups were different. High birth order, uneven parental discipline, average or above-average IQ, and bad job performance are all characteristics of organized criminals. It is common for organized criminals to be socially skilled and live with a partner. Before the murder, he may have described himself as furious, but thereafter, he may have described himself as comfortable and at peace. Before, during, and after the murder of an organized killer, the crime scene seems to be in order. It is common for the victim to be a stranger, and

they may be singled out because of where they are or what they are wearing. OCD-like conduct and crime scene patterns are seen in the behavior and patterns of the organized killer. For their part, disorganized criminals tend to be less intelligent, come from lower social ranks, and have endured harsher forms of discipline from their parents. At the time of the murder, he is emotionally disturbed, socially inept, and sexually unfit. Observing the crime scene, it is clear that the perpetrators had no strategy in place to avoid discovery. Facial disfigurement and sexually degrading behavior are not uncommon following a homicide. It is common for criminals who are not organized to leave the victim's corpse in the same position in which they were slain. There are also real-life examples and images to illustrate the points being made.

Serial killers in this category are the hardest to catch. They tend to be very bright and precise in their planning and execution. The murderer meticulously plans out every aspect of the crime and takes every effort to ensure that no evidence is left behind. This sort of psychopath is known to keep an eye out for possible victims for days on end to identify someone they believe would be easy prey. Once the victim has been selected, the assassin will abduct them and transport them to a new place where they will be murdered, generally using some type of trick to earn their sympathy. It is common for murderers to take efforts to guarantee that the victim's corpse is not discovered until they want it to be. Typically, a criminal of this kind takes tremendous pleasure in his or her "job" and pays careful attention to news headlines about the crimes he or she has committed. They may be driven by a desire to frustrate investigators working to solve the case.

It is unusual for these killers to plot out their victims' killings in any manner. Most of the time, the victims of their crimes are just unlucky. Initially, it seems that this kind of serial killer takes advantage of every chance that comes to his want law enforcement, but they don't cover their trails. As a rule, violent criminals who are disorganized have low IQs and exhibit high antisocialist. They have few, if any, close friends or family members and tend to move around a lot. These assassins are prone to confessing that they were propelled to do their crimes by voices in their brains or some other fictitious source even if they don't remember doing so.

An extensive multidimensional scaling approach was used to determine the degree to which the 39 different elements were present in each other. An examination of the data found that there are no distinguishable subsets of crime features that are linked to the organization or disorganization of the murders, as this research demonstrated. A subset of ordered traits is seen in most serial homicides, but disorderly features are significantly less common and do not seem to represent a different kind of serial killer. The recommended testing typologies to support the expert opinion and increase our understanding of crime are provided in general terms. It seems unlikely that using a template to specify the properties of a certain type would be supported by research. Even though typology has a general weakness, the organized/disorganized dichotomy is of particular interest since it is the only one that can be tested against other related typologies, such as the four-fold 'cardinal humor' type, which is now just historical.

- The concept of a "mixed" category raises substantial issues about whether or not the basic divide can be experimentally proven. If a large percentage of real-world circumstances are mixed,' this basic difference is unlikely to hold up. Only a theoretical proposal, with no practical application. As part of criminal investigation and crime scene classification, it's important to know the origin and status of the reports used. Rather than relying on scholarly publications to disseminate scientific information, authors are increasingly turning to popular novels, which are written for an audience that is neither technical nor expert. As a result, in a professional or academic context, it is unlikely to get the critical study it needs. It is more likely to be accepted by law enforcement professionals who are not trained in science than by those who are.

- Theories and models presented in widely distributed films and given more credibility as a consequence of their extensive dissemination may be accepted by juries and other lay groups as part of an acknowledged body of knowledge as a result of this process. This may also lead to the possibility that the principles may be implemented recklessly and used less meticulously original authors had planned.

- The organized/disorganized dichotomy has surely been cited in several Hollywood blockbusters as a paradigm for police investigations worldwide. A key reason the dichotomy is intriguing, according to some sources, is because it was established as part of attempts to identify the "gritty psychological aspects of a person" by examining their criminal past and providing a general picture of them. To put it another way, the site of the crime is inspected to see whether it was well-planned or randomly committed. According to this theory, organized criminals will carry out organized crime, whereas disorganized acts criminals will carry out dispose of organized crime. This duality is a major paradigm when it comes to establishing conclusions about offenders.

- The Organized/Disorganized typology has been widely accepted as a conceptual framework for police investigations, "offender profiling." Despite its extensive use, the philosophy and concepts of the two-fold model seem to be inadequately described. It has a misty feel about it, too.

- indication that Stones' comprehensive research of serial homicide's inception supports any difference between "organized" and "disorganized" perpetrators. The key distinction is that this is still a proposal that has to be well developed and evaluated. The two-fold typology seems to have been influenced by a "syndrome" or "illness" method of categorization, however, its philosophical origins remain murky. This strategy places everyone in the framework of the category into a single group. This assignment is based on the fact that subcategory members have a common set of features. These qualities may be used to determine whether or not a person has or is displaying signs and symptoms of a certain sickness or condition by offering a template of features. In the early 1900s, this method faced several obstacles, especially when applied to human behavior. Statistics and psychometrics have been spawned by the development of new techniques to categorize individuals based on empirical data.

MEDICAL KILLER

When we are at our weakest and most vulnerable, the medical experts we turn to for aid undergo extensive training before they are allowed to treat and care for the people under their care. These doctors and their patients share a degree of trust and responsibility that is uncommon in human interactions. 'Angel of compassion murders,' as they were called in the early years, were common. Some of the perpetrators of these acts believe they are doing it to alleviate the pain of their victims.

A patient's suffering is a requirement in many situations, but it's not always the case, and it's not unusual for a perpetrator to increase their victim pool based on this criteria over time.

These crimes are made possible, it seems, by easy access to pharmaceuticals, with poisoning being the most often used means of death, with insulin accounting for the vast majority of the instances examined. There was just one example in the research when the victim was poisoned and suffocated at the same time. Mental health concerns and personality disorder symptoms were found in more than half the 16 criminals evaluated.

The fact that the nurse was on duty at the time of all of the homicides has been regarded as a key piece of evidence in several instances, according to the report. The fact that they were present in the hospital at the time of the fatalities is not enough to establish their culpability, however; this is an unacceptable

situation were sentenced to a minimum of 35 years in prison for two murders and 19 poisonings. Chua, who was convicted in May 2015, maintains his innocence, stating that he is innocent and spent his life in jail There are now suspicions that a total of ten more fatalities occurred while Victorino Chua was working at the hospital as a result of the foul activity.

However, even in 94% of the 16 serial killer nurse instances reviewed, the mortality rate during those nurses' shifts was greater than usual, stressing the need to look forward for ot utilizing one such quality or characteristic to accuse one person.

COMMON SIGNS OF SERIAL KILLERS:

It's easy to dismiss serial murderers as horrible freaks of nature. There must be telltale indicators of a serial murderer, don't you think? They're not like the rest of us. A distinct kind of creature, with characteristics and a life expectancy that is completely out of the ordinary for human beings. This isn't always the case, however. Every day, serial murderers walk among us, attending the same schools and jobs as we do, reading the same news, and having the same beliefs as us. They're just like us. They hide in plain sight by seeming to be normal human beings and blending in with the rest of the population. Serial killers may, sometimes, let their masks fall.

For example, you may have heard the phrases "psychopathic," "sociopath," and "narcissistic" used when discussing serial murderers because these personality disorders (and many more) are widespread among serial killers. This implies that they'll show signs of these diseases in their behavior, which makes it easier for us to identify them.

People who are most likely to become serial murderers may be recognized by following a few basic guidelines. The murderers' violent conduct may be predicted by these characteristics, but they are not directly connected to the serial activity.

A person's extreme antisocial conduct may be a sign that he or she has a mental health issue, but it is not a guarantee. The Diagnostic and Statistical Manual of Mental Disorders (DSM-IV-TR) describes someone with antisocial personality disorder as having no sense of regret or guilt for their actions. Some of the most common symptoms of antisocial personality disorder are dishonesty (including deception), aggression, a lack of regard for social standards, and lack of accountability.

Voyeurism in young individuals may be an early sign of psychopathic inclinations. Serial murderers sometimes aim for total dominion over their victims, and seeing them in secret may give some individuals a feeling of power. This is a characteristic that many serial murderers display from a young age forward.

Setting fires is one of the most typical warning signals that serial murderers demonstrate. It is not uncommon for young individuals to like the sight of a fire, but a psychopath's passion crosses the line into arsonist territory.' To get rid of anything, they'll do everything they can to set it on fire.

In addition to killing or hurting animals, this is a typical sign of probable serial killing behavior. Other animals may be abused or even killed because of their activities, such as cats and dogs The individual will not display any guilt or regret even after realizing the consequences of their conduct. Slaying a little animal, such as a puppy or kitten, is a relatively easy task for a serial killer since they are so young and inexperienced. It is very dangerous for any kid who engages in this kind of behavior to grow up to be a serial murderer in the future.

Some Common Traits Of Serial Killers Are

ABSENCE OF COMPASSION:

The lack of emotional depth is one of the most typical traits of serial murderers. Empathy stands out. An act of planned murder cannot be committed while feeling empathy for the victim. Like Bundy, most murderers have individuals in t heir life who appear to care about them more tha n just their agendas.

In prison, Bundy claimed that he loved the female he was with and that he really liked thei r time together, and she also indicated that he was always attentive and considerate toward her and her child.

Because it places a greater gap between severely prohibited conduct and what we'd term "normal behavior," I believe this presumption that there's no empathy plays a role. People like Bundy may be able to sense empathy but yet have powerful needs that force them to act on their desires, regardless of any other misgivings they may have. In my opinion, a big percentage of society might be categorized as lacking empathy for strangers based on how they behave and feel toward immigrants and refugees.

dunno, I simply don't think it's usually an adequate explanation for people's conduct, but I do believe that many murderers lack empathy fully or at least in major part.
Also, I'm baffled as to why a lack of empathy would compel someone to engage in violent conduct.

To the best of my knowledge, the absence of empathy is a rather neutral emotional state, similar to indifference. If you don't care or can't comprehend what other people are feeling, it doesn't mean you want to hurt them, in my opinion. The fact that you're not empathic doesn't mean you can't be friendly to someone, or at the very least contemptuous of them.
When it comes to social growth, the capacity to

put oneself in someone else's shoes is a vital s

kill that must be learned.

Psychopaths are known for their inability to emp

athize with others, especially their victims, re

gularly. offenders with mental conditions are m

ore likely to re-offend the

following release from prison.

Psychopathy is a mental illness characterized by

 a lack of empathy, a tendency to deceive others

, and an inability to feel regret for one's acti

ons. criminals' empathy response, known as the m

irror system, fires up the same way it does in c

ontrols only when scientists urge them to empath

ize.

They demonstrate decreased activity in the areas of t he brain linked with pain when they are not taught.

To engage our mirror neurons while watching

or doing a task, we use the term "mirror system

," which refers to our brain's mirror neuronsThe

y're regarded to be essential for developing emp

athy for others. The majority of serial

murderers have this feature, which is widespread

in both sociopaths and psychopaths. Even if a

serial murderer lacks empathy for everyone and

everything, this does not mean that he or she lacks empathy for everything and everyone.

Serial killers are capable of showing empathy for another person

Even if that person does not end up as one of their victims. Research shows serial murderers are aware of their victims' misery, but they don't experience it themselves. As a serial murderer, you're expected to be cold and unfeeling toward your victims; this is a well-known stereotype of a killer, particularly one who has committed several crimes. They are not human beings. They lack aspirations, ambitions, and aspirations in their lives. They have no relatives or friends who will be saddened by their death. They have no concept of misery or agony. To the monster, they're just another way to get what they want.

The universal human capacity for empathy, primarily by contrasting the physiology and behavior of "normal" people with that of those who have committed murder or other heinous acts against another. Diagnostic categories for a wide range of mental health problems have been developed in psychology. Narcissistic disorder, bipolar disorder, and antisocial personality disorder all fall under this category. Illness all have been linked to reduced capacity for empathy (BPD). The lack of empathy may only endure for a brief period or may even be transitory in certain cases. This personality disorder is the most often linked to serious criminality of the three mentioned.

- Many'mirrorr' neurons in the brain have been found by neuroscientists, and they are engaged when a person sees and does the identical action at the same time. Watching someone else do something activates our brains in the same manner as doing the same thing yourself.

- The possibility that humans might "reconstruct" the experiences of others points to the existence of a brain toolbox designed for this particular purpose. Neuroscientists used the same fMRI equipment to scan the brains of 121 inmates in a medium-security prison to better understand the absence of empathy in this population. Visual images showing physical pain, such as those depicting an injured finger or an imprisoned toe, were requested for inmates. After that, the inmates were asked to visualize themselves in the same situations shown in the photos that they had been shown before. They also had to imagine what it would be like to be in someone else's shoes. After that, they were shown scenes in which there was no discomfort, such as a hand resting on a doorknob.

- Using the conventional PCL-R diagnostic approach for assessing psychopathic traits, the offenders were divided into three groups of almost equal size. High, moderate, and low levels of psychopath were found. It turns out that, when tested to see how they would react under pain, individuals in the most psychopathic subgroup behaved just like anybody else. Pain-sensitive areas of the brain include the right amygdala, the somatosensory cortex, the anterior insular, and the anterior midcingulate cortex. When you're in pain, the opposite is true.

- As with the idea of suffering imposed on someone else, self-inflicted pain engaged the same parts of the brain. These people's ventral striatum, a pleasure center, was stimulated when they contemplated the pain of others. This was an alarming discovery.

IMPULSIVENESS WITHOUT REMORSE

Serial murderers have always piqued the public's curiosity due to the almost limitless number of victims they can take care of before feeling any regret, sorrow, or self-control. As they creep along invisibly, they can carry on their atrocities for a very long time, all over the world. As a continuation of my previous research on serial killers, I intend to expand my previous study with more cases and more background information about the roots of their amok from both a psychological and a biological perspective. This study will focus on serial killers' amok from both a psychological and a biological perspective. The amygdala's role in enhancing aggressive behavior and contributing to uncontrolled sadism will also be examined.

Childhood traumas, humiliation, and neglect have a profound effect on a person's life, as well as their family history. These are some of the most well-known psychopaths, and I have grouped their commonalities into categories. Many additional aspects play a part in a person's success, such as their superiority, their ability to manipulate others, their impairment in physical attributes, or their need for pleasure, profit, or attention. Being self-absorbed and possessing an addictive personality may all lead to murders according to experts so This is related to the previous statement. Remember that serial murderer rarely has any regret for what they've done. If they had done so, they would not have been referred to as 'serials.'

Law enforcement, the individuals they serve, and the rest of society all benefit from researching and resolving cold cases. First and first, the well-being of the community is the most important consideration. When criminals are sentenced to prison, the community is spared their misdeeds and its residents are given a greater sense of security. Both real and perceived safety are intertwined. Businesses might be harmed if customers avoid certain times and locations because they are afraid of the consequences of unsolved crimes on their customers' mental health and financial stability. The acts of serial offenders are compounded by their celebrity, and with each unsolved case, there is an increased sense of omnipresent danger in society. Second, and no less important, is the sense of justice that victims feel when their perpetrators are brought to justice. 1 It is very uncommon for survivors and their families to assume that law enforcement has abandoned them. 2 Law enforcement has a moral obligation to carry out its responsibilities, and settling cold cases boosts public confidence in the department. It's not only about boosting public safety and justice; it's about saving a lot of money. In the United States alone, crime costs are estimated to be between $690 billion to $3.41 trillion each year. Many factors contribute to the costs of crime for victims, including the costs of reacting to crimes, conducting investigations, and incarcerating suspects, including attempts at crime prevention and the immediate consequences of crimes, such as medical and burial expenses.

Intangible costs to victims and the community are even more difficult to calculate. Emotional costs can never be quantified, but fear and post-traumatic reactions may be quantified if psychological aid and physical security measures are computed.

There have been several serial murderers who have challenged this tendency, with some stating that they had learned to feel regret after a sufficient period had passed. Considering that many serial murderers are adept at hiding their genuine motives, it's hard to tell for sure whether this is anything more than a ruse. There is a consensus that serial murderers lack remorse, and all other assertions are created for their profit by psychologists and criminal mind experts. I should be killed for what I have done" and Edmund Kemper's decision to turn himself in are outliers, both situations are very unusual (and possibly another form of manipulation).

IMPULSIVENESS

Having said that, the "disorganized" offenders (despite this being a very wide phrase) are the most likely to demonstrate poor impulse control. These are the ruthless, opportunistic murderers who can't help but take advantage of whatever opportunity they see. In his maniacal quest to amass a collection of the eyeballs of his victims, Charles Albright was a prolific serial murderer.

Humans have always been able to kill each other. In warfare, some did it out of rage, fear, envy, or sheer greed for money, while others found smaller motivations. Humans have murdered for drugs, for money, and in self-defense or for the protection of others. But murderers, those who commit crimes against humanity, are to blame.

The predatory murderer (those who meticulously plan and premeditate their crimes) was shown to have no substantial cognitive or intellectual impairments, whereas the impulsive killer was found to be more mentally impaired, especially cognitively impaired. According to the investigation, a large number of the "planners" had some kind of mental illness. The planners were also twice as likely to have a mental problem as the impulse killer.

Most of the impulsive murderers had a history of drug or alcohol misuse or were under the influence of these substances at the time of their murders, which is unusual. About three-quarters of the people involved in the planning process were dependent on or abusing drugs or alcohol in some way. instead, instead of the mindless murdering robots, we see in slashed movies.

There is no escaping the fact that fictional bad guys are human (at least in the majority of mystery and thriller stories) and must have a distinct personality, good or bad. The reader must have access to the character's human attributes to form an opinion about him or her.

There was no need for me to view this study's findings to predict what would happen. When it comes to murder and other crimes, I think most detectives will agree with me when I say that drug and alcohol misuse is a major factor.

On the other hand, some murderers can control their impulses. These are the psychopaths who follow their victims for days or weeks before the assault and meticulously prepare every detail of their depraved deed.

The BTK Killer, for example, was well-known for spending weeks or months observing and studying the patterns of his victims before carrying out an assault. When it came to IQ and other aspects of cognitive function, impulsive killers were much less capable than those who were not "the predatory and premeditated murders did not often have any severe intellectual or cognitive deficiencies, but far more of them had mental illnesses."

An online journal article published in Criminal Justice and Behavior examines the neuropsychological and intellectual difference between killers who kill impulsively and those who kill as the consequence of an organized strategy.

Premeditated murderers are nearly twice as likely as impulsive killers to have a history of mood disorders or psychotic illnesses—61 percent against 34 percent.

59 percent of impulsive killers had developmental disabilities and cognitive and intellectual impairments, compared to 36 percent of predatory murderers.

Those who murder on the spur of the moment are much more likely to have a history of substance addiction and/or be under the influence of alcohol or drugs at the time of the crime (93 percent vs 76 percent).

Seventy-seven murders from the general population of Illinois and Missouri were categorized into two categories (impulsive and premeditated killers) based on established criteria. When Hanlon examined their results on standardized IQ tests and neuropsychological memory, attention, and executive function tests, he discovered some interesting results. He took his time with each person, going through a battery of tests to get a full picture of their condition. Thousands of hours have been invested by Hanlon in his investigation into the thoughts of killers. There must be more research into the mental health of those who perpetrate these crimes, to better understand their cognitive processes and the psychopathology, neuropathy, and other mental disorders," he said. "Ultimately, we may be able to boost our rates of prevention and aid the courts, especially in assisting judges and juries in better understanding the minds and mental anomalies of the persons who perpetrate these violent crimes

GRANDIOSITY

Even though I'm focusing on female serial killers in my true crime project, I've unearthed a lot of material regarding male serial killers as well, even though my focus is on the latter. Serial murderers had 23 physical anomalies, according to research by Joel Norris Ph.D. Despite the differing viewpoints of several experts, determining whether someone will or will not commit serial murder is not a simple matter. A wide range of elements must be taken into accounts, such as psychological and neurological problems as well as environmental and social problems, as well as injury to the prefrontal lobes or the frontal cortex.

Randomness is one of the most terrifying aspects of serial murderers. Some serial murderers seem to be the "average Joe," one of the millions of "ordinary Joes" who don't turn out to be cruel murderers. They chose their victims at random, and many individuals who know serial killers characterize them as such. However, you may be relieved to realize that most serial murderers have qualities that distinguish them from the rest of the population. Without knowing someone who possesses all of the above attributes, you're probably not going to feel much better.

A large percentage of serial murderers have a mental condition. An antisocial personality or psychopathy may be to blame. Nature vs. nurture is the distinction between the two: The impulse control and emotional areas of the brain of a psychopath are undeveloped from birth. Antisocial personalities, on the other hand, are ingrained in people from a young age, frequently as a result of abuse or neglect. People must show that they were unable to distinguish between good and wrong when they committed their acts to be labeled as criminally insane. Serial murderers are perfectly aware of right and wrong, but they don't give a damn.

As "sociopaths," those who suffer from an antisocial personality disorder "have no concern for good and wrong," which is a trait shared by serial killers, as well as those who lack remorse, are callous, and act impulsively. However, not all sociopaths are violent murderers. The great majority of them aren't even murderers. Although the sociopath in your neighborhood may not pose a risk to you, you should avoid falling for his or her attractions at all costs.

Physicality alone isn't enough to characterize our activities. This list of 23 serial murderer physical anomalies is only a sliver of the bigger picture. The total of these factors encourages the development of multiple killers. You'll be on the lookout for these irregularities in everyone you come across after reading this list. As long as you can tick one of these boxes for yourself, your family members, or friends, don't worry. As I previously said, serial murderers' physical deformities are just a small portion of the whole. It's impossible to know who has violent inclinations or not. In the end, that's what makes free will so wonderful. The ability to live a peaceful, crime-free existence is within our reach, even if we are genetically prone to serial homicide. Some of us, for whatever reason, aren't able to.

SOME OF THE ABNORMALITIES ARE

- Fingers with rounded tips
- Inconvenient hair that won't comb itself
- Hair that is easily tangled and goes astray when combed
- Curly locks
- Head circumference is large (outside the norm of 1.5 cm or less)
- Eyelids that connect at the nose are known as epicanthus (the point of union is deeply covered or partially covered)

- Hyperteliorism is characterized by an abnormally large or small space between the tear ducts.

- Ears that sit lower than the corner of the eye and nose bridge—the top point where the ear meets the head is lower than.5 cm or higher than.5 cm lower than the corner of the eye and nose bridge.

- Ears that are deformed

- Low-hanging earlobes that stick out in a way that draws attention to the crown of the head

- Ears that are very flexible or squishy

- Palate with a lot of muscle

- Steep or flat and thin, the roof of the mouth is unquestionably present.

- Deep ridges on the front of the tongue

- The tongue is speckled with either smooth or rough patches.

- There may be a distinct curvature of the fifth finger toward the other fingers or a faint claw-like curvature.

- In palmistry the "heart line" and "headline" are two distinct lines that are fused into one single transverse palmer crease (a single crease that extends across the palm).

- The third toe is either longer or the same length as the second toe.

- 2nd and 3rd middle toes partially syndactyly zed

- Between the first and second toes, the space is wider than typical.

- Injuries to the teeth

- Dermatoglyphic anomalies (skin texture)

NARCISSISM

Narcissism, or an exaggerated view of one's importance, often goes hand in hand with a person's tendency toward grandiosity. For most serial murderers, the perception of their crimes is of utmost importance to them, hence they may try to influence the narratives of their stories. Those seeking attention aren't ashamed to make public displays of their criminality. Later, he bragged about the crime in chat forums, even going so far as to publish images of his work to show other self-proclaimed cannibals. Killers are known to leave notes at murder sites or contact the media directly to establish their aliases.

Oftentimes, serial murderers admit their crimes to guarantee that their identities are associated with them. Having their name carved in the annals of real crime is what matters to them.' As early as 1886, serial murder was identified as a psychopathological disease. Theories on what drives serial killers are as diverse as the people who possess such features and characteristics. It's been argued that trauma in childhood and sexual dysfunction and neurobiological abnormalities are all factors that contribute to the development of PTSD. Serial homicide and pathological narcissism have been connected in the past fifteen years as narcissism has been examined more extensively. Narcissistic personality disorder (NPD), narcissistic damage, emotions of inadequacy and humiliation, self-glorifying fantasies, and underlying sentiments of inadequacy have all been linked to serial killers. As an example, the following case study includes a discussion of clinical research, theory, and

While serial murderers tend to influence their victims, they are equally adept at ensuring that you are unaware of this. For the most part, we want to think of horror as occurring only in movies and to other people. As a result, we assume that the person we just met or the person who lives next door can't possibly be wicked. It was simpler for him to accept the falsehoods than confess that his kid was a monster, so he took them at their face value.

Even those of us who aren't in a romantic connection with a potentially hazardous someone may be influenced. It's crucial to be on the watch for those who exude a superficial charm that might fool anybody into thinking they're safe.

You should be wary of anybody who tries to flatter you or divert your attention with presents, especially if those activities seem to be intended to hide anything, such as holes in a tale, the whereabouts of a lost item, or a peculiar favor or demand. You need to be aware of your weaknesses to protect yourself against psychopaths.

A person's body and mind, a sacred temple, and a familiar landscape of sensation and personal history are the only places where one's privacy, intimacy, integrity, and inviolability are assured. A desecrated temple is invaded and defiled by the perpetrator. To his undisguised delight, he does it in public, on purpose, repeatedly, and often in a sadistic and sexual manner. As a result, abuse has long-lasting and sometimes irreparable consequences and effects.

In a sense, the victim's own body and psyche become his greatest adversaries. The sufferer's mental and physical anguish is what forces him to change, lose his sense of self, and let up on his beliefs and convictions. In the hands of a bully or tormentor, one's body and brain become a traitorous, poisoned domain, an unbreakable communication route. As a result, the victim of abuse becomes humiliatingly reliant on the abuser. The victim incorrectly believes that his degradation and dehumanization are directly linked to the denial of his bodily necessities, such as contact, light, sleep, the toilet, food, water, and safety. As he sees it, he is become bestial by his own body and awareness, not by the vicious bullies around him.

MANIPULATIONS

If you're a person who believes that the whole world is a cesspool of depravity, you're not alone. I'm talking about Aileen Worms, the woman accused of killing seven men.

A serial killer's psyche has long been a mystery, a subject of investigation. Some argue that it's a sickness, while others argue that it's the result of childhood trauma. Despite our lack of understanding of why serial murderers commit their heinous crimes, one thing we have learned is that most of them are quite likable. Because of this, they utilize their charm to establish trust in their victims and entice them into their deadly ruse. That's impressive. While serial murderers tend to influence their victims, they are equally adept at ensuring that you are unaware of this. Serial criminals, particularly those who engage in rape and murder sprees, often do so to elicit an emotional response. "Sensation seeking" behavior is the name given to this kind of behavior.

People who suffer from mental illness or abuse as a kid may develop a sense of powerlessness, which is a dangerous defect for someone who can use violence. Those who believe they have little power over their own lives and circumstances tend to seek smaller, more controllable aspects of their life over which they may exert total authority. In a situation when the individual lacks empathy, that region may include other people.

, a person's prior experiences aren't only responsible for the development of an out-of-control desire for power. It might be difficult for children whose families are unstable to form close friendships with their classmates since they don't have much time to do so, making it even more difficult for them to feel in control of their life. In addition to their control difficulties, they also lack empathy since they don't have

LUST OF POWER

Many companions with whom they may learn and build the empathy that all normal human beings have. Lack of empathy and the drive to dominate people is a fatal mix.

As with all serial murderers, their motives for killing are unique. Hedonistic desire is a motive for certain assassins. Others are driven by avarice or a need for adrenaline rushes. The power/control murderer is one of the most typical types of a serial killers. These serial murderers are driven by a desire to control and dominate their victims as their main goal. They take pleasure in the act of killing. Because they like pursuing, catching, and tormenting their victim, they are predatory. The act of murder is usually the most fulfilling and ultimate display of their power and control over their victims, not just because it is sexually appealing to them. They are slow killers who enjoy torturing and killing their victims for the sheer enjoyment of it.

The mutilating attack is what sets apart the lust murder committed by the organized nonsocial and disorganized social person. A nonsocial type feeling rejected by and hated by the society in which they live. Lust murder is the least expression of his unconditional hate. In contrast, the disorganized associative type also harbors feelings of resentment at the world, but only expresses these feelings in the murder of a loved one. The position of the victim's corpse, indications of torture or mutilation before the appearance of physical evidence at the murder site may all indicate the personality type engaged in a lust murder. The murder was premeditated, although the victim was unknown to the perpetrator. Psychological profiling may be useful in certain situations, however

A homicide committed out of romantic compulsion is known as a lust murder.

Erotophonophilia, or sexual arousal or enjoyment based on the death of a human person, is a synonym for lust murder. Victims' sexual organs or other parts of their body are often cut or mutilated in this sort of crime, which is often committed while the victim is engaged in sexual intercourse. The victim's genitalia may be eviscerated and/or relocated during the mutilation. In most cases, the mutilation occurs after death. Such behaviors as removing clothes, posing and supporting the body in various sexual postures, inserting items into bodily orifices, anthropophagic, and necrophilia may be included. The majority of passion murders are committed by men, however, there have been reports of female lust killers. Serial murderers are more likely than others to commit acts of desired murder. In the minds of these criminals, a link between the murder and sexual pleasure has been established. It must be something about the victim that the offender finds sexually appealing for this sort of offender to pick them as a victim. In the offender's Ideal Victim Type, this appealing quality may be found in all of the offender's victims. An offender may pass over numerous prospective targets because they do not fit his IVT. To carry out his fantasies on his victim, the perpetrator may engage in stalking or other predatory activity after finding a suitable victim. In passion murders, fantasies play an important role, although they can never be fully realized. Throughout the film, the desire killer's dream will change and get more brutal as he attempts to fulfill it.

Unlike hedonists who desire murderers, many power/control killers rape their victims for reasons other than lust. Rape, on the other hand, is a method through which predators exert dominance and control over their prey. Unlike thrill murderers like the Zodiac, power/control killers do not lose interest in their victims after they are dead. Long after a victim has been murdered, a power/control murderer may return to have sex with the rotting body to ensure his dominance and control over the dead. Officer Tim Boyle of the Des Plaines Police Department The late John Wayne Gacy Author's Note: Tim Boyle, Des Plaines Police Department

As with all serial murderers, their motives for killing are unique. Hedonistic desire is a motive for certain assassins. Others are driven by avarice or a need for adrenaline rushes. The power/control murderer is one of the most typical types of a serial killers.

These serial murderers are driven by a desire to control and dominate their victims as their main goal. They take pleasure in the act of killing. Because they like pursuing, catching, and tormenting their victim, they are predatory. The act of murder is usually the most fulfilling and ultimate display of their power and control over their victims, not just because it is sexually appealing to them. They are slow killers who enjoy torturing and killing their victims for the sheer enjoyment of it.

While outwardly committing his crimes, BTK was secretly satiating his sexual desires and postponing his urge to kill for months or even years at a time via autoerotic fantasies and masturbation in which he relived his murders using trophies seized from his victims.

The " category of predators includes power/control murderers because they are careful planners, unflappable, and patient. Charismatic, charismatic, and brilliant are all words that come to mind when describing these types of serial murderers. Unlike hedonists who desire murderers, many power/control killers rape their victims for reasons other than lust. Rape, on the other hand, is a method through which predators exert dominance and control over their prey. Unlike thrill murderers like the Zodiac, power/control killers do not lose interest in their victims after they are dead. Long after a victim has been murdered, a power/control murderer may return to have sex with the rotting body to ensure his dominance and control over the death. Power/control killers can return to their victims anytime they want since necrophilia completely removes the prospect of the victim rejecting them. So, rather than being rejected and disappointed by a real person, a psychopath who commits serial killings might feel that he or she is in control of the situation.

SENSATION SEEKING:

I believe I've come across a serial murderer in the past. I know two persons who fit these requirements. How many times does a person murder before they are caught? One of them once asked me this question. When I meet someone who is both charming and low-key, I can't help but worry about their motives. He satisfies the prerequisites. As a result of childhood brain injuries, another guy I know is obsessed with power and control. Tends to deviate from the norm. I'm being followed. The second one, in particular, sends shivers down my spine. A dream followed. In a dream, I saw my spouse dispose of a woman's corpse in the woods, and I was horrified. As he turned around, he took a peek at me. He has every one of them. He's tried to murder me in the past as well. We've been cut off. p.o. Now that I've had these reoccurring dreams, I'm curious to know... Is my city a hotbed for the disappearance of women? Because of this, I went to a missing people site More than a dozen women who look like me and are 5'5 to 5'6" and a little overweight has gone missing in the previous year. There was a striking resemblance in both their ethnicity and clothing between them and myself. I'm becoming more alarmed. My ex-girlfriend is probably a serial murderer. It's impossible to confirm or disprove. He's been following and spying on her for the past year. In a risk assessment quiz for women who have been abused, my score was? To my surprise, the message "Extreme Danger" had returned! Because he has hacked into my email, I am unable to access it. I'm sure he's doing his homework. There are a few individuals who I feel are on the verge of breaking the law. Even while they may never really murder, they are exceedingly cold and manipulative, preying on their victims. Psychopaths and sociopaths have several features, including a lack of remorse or empathy for others, a lack of shame or capacity to accept responsibility for their acts, a disrespect for laws or social standards, and a predisposition to violence. A basic aspect of both is a deceptive and manipulative disposition. But how can we tell them apart?

Sociopaths are generally less emotionally stable and very impulsive — Their behavior is more disorganized than that of psychopaths. Sociopaths are more likely to act out of compulsion when they commit crimes, whether they are violent or nonviolent. And they will be impatient, succumbing to impulsiveness and lack of careful planning much more swiftly.

In contrast, psychopaths meticulously plot their crimes and take calculated risks to avoid detection. The savvy ones will leave few signs that may lead to getting caught. Psychopaths don't get carried away in the present and make fewer errors as a consequence.

Both operate on a continuum of behavior, and many psychologists still question whether the two should be distinguished at all. But for those who do discriminate between the two, one thing is widely agreed upon: psychiatrists use the word psychopath to demonstrate that the etiology of the anti-social personality disorder is inherited. Sociopath defines behavior that is the outcome of a brain lesion, or abuse and/or neglect in infancy

Psychopaths are born and sociopaths are created. In essence, their divergence illustrates the nature vs. nurture issues

HOMICIDES OCCURRENCE:

The causes for some of these horrifying acts of violence have yet to be proven, but some informed assumptions have been made. "Various theses of the etiology of serial murder exist, the majority of which choose to fit with a psychiatric, social, or biological etiology," says one researcher. What is it in a man that causes him to become so twisted that he commits murder? The McDonald Triad refers to a set of three factors that are linked to serial homicide. Teenage serial murderers exhibit three distinct traits, which are known as the triad, in their early years. There are three common childhood diagnoses among "typical" serial killers: pyromania, chronic bedwetting, and cruelty to animals. Do we have the ability to prevent serial murders before they happen? A biological explanation for his correlations is most likely, but the three features he identified are also linked to a history of oppression in society.

We can compare murder rates between nations and across time using death rates.

Death rates are not affected by changes in other causes or risk factors for death, unlike the proportion of deaths that we analyzed before.

For a specific nation or area, the number of deaths per 100,000 inhabitants is known as the mortality rate. What becomes apparent is the wide disparity in mortality rates across Latin. In the United States, the mortality rate per 100,000 people is often more than 30; in El Salvador, it was above 45. There were less than 1 killing per 100,000 people in Western Europe, Japan, or the Middle East compared to these countries.

A 50-fold increase in disparity. Homicide is an issue that is unique to each nation. Homicide rates are quite low in several nations throughout the globe. However, killings may be a frequent occurrence for certain people. Historians and archivists are needed to understand how murder rates evolved before the contemporary age. Historical Violence Database: A collection of statistics on long-term patterns in homicide rates, as well as qualitative information such as the perpetrator's identity, victim's identity, and the cause of death. Only nations with extensive historical records on violence and crime are included in this database, namely those in Western Europe and the US.

Some European areas have maintained police records of persons accused of murder or manslaughter since the second part of the nineteenth century, as well as yearly homicide victim statistics.

Eisner compiled estimates of murder rates from over ninety academic articles, going back to the thirteenth century, to see how long people had been killing one other. The long-term murder rates for five European areas are displayed in this graph. The Historical Violence Database and Eisner's (2003) article are used to calculate homicide rates before 1990, which are expressed as the number of homicides per 100,000 people. Homicide rates from the Global Burden of Disease research have been integrated with these estimates starting in 1990.

As in Latin America today, murder rates in Western Europe in the 1300s varied from 23 to 56 per 100,000 people. From the 1300s to the 1800s, homicide rates dropped considerably in all five areas. Homicide rates dropped by 78 to 98 percent in most nations, which was comparable across the board. Europe's homicide rate has dropped significantly in recent years. When it comes to Europe's economic decline, the early 2000s were the worst for England, Germany,

Switzerland, and Italy; the mid-to-late 1900s were the worst for the Netherlands, Belgium, and Scandinavia, respectively.

REACTIVE MEASURES OF SERIAL KILLERS

There have also been several reactive methods for capturing serial murderers throughout history. Criminal profiling is the most popular. Profiling is used to apprehend a murderer after he has already committed the crime, as opposed to the preceding approaches, which aim to deter future serial murderers. It's a method for narrowing down the possible suspects in a case to people who share particular traits. Based on studies, these characteristics have been seen in other criminals of a similar kind. The goal of profiling is not to identify a particular culprit, but rather to provide investigators with a general concept of what to look for in a suspect. The Investigative Support Units had a major role in the long-term evolution of this strategy, although parts of it had been in operation long before then. Thomas Bond examined one of Jack the Ripper's victims. Bond recommended that police seek a "calm, inoffensive appearing individual, presumably middle-aged and properly dressed" owing to the nature of the evidence. Although there is a lot of buzz about new criminal profiling tools, they have been around for a while. Using profiling methods has helped law enforcement agencies catch numerous criminals, and as they get more refined, the procedure becomes increasingly more successful in identifying prospective suspects. While it is critical to enhance profile accuracy to catch killers, proactive strategies to intervene before a killing occurs may be more crucial to our society's future.

When looking into a series of homicides, the National Integrated Ballistics Identification Network (NIBIN) is often used. This database focuses on bullets and cartridges, unlike earlier ones. Comparing evidence from multiple crime scenes is made easier with this imaging technology. Professionals may use it to determine whether a murder was committed with the same weapon, which enables them to assume that a certain perpetrator is involved.

When the police get a call and learn that something has occurred, they initiate a reactive investigation. Sole after concluding that a murder has been committed they begin to act. This is the only method by which they learned that there was a case to be investigated. In the case of serial murderers, anticipating their future moves is critical. If only evidence at the crime site is examined, specialists can't prevent future crimes and rescue prospective victims, particularly if they are chosen at random.

In dealing with serial killers, numerous investigative tactics might be employed to overcome the obstacles associated with this undertaking. Reactive police investigations are the norm, and they deal only with crimes that have already been committed. But when serial murderers are involved, proactive measures must be taken to avoid future atrocities and forecast the killer's next moves. The use of informants, intelligence, and other databases that provide case-specific data might all be considered options for the police in this regard.

INDEPENDENT ANALYSIS OF SERIAL KILLERS

Our society has been aware of the prevalence of the crime of murder. In their comprehensive investigations into the issue of murder, historians have discovered evidence that the crime occurred as early as Roman times and has persisted through the ages. Jack the Ripper, who murdered and disfigured five prostitutes in London's East End in 1888, was one of the earliest contemporary instances of what would be considered a serial murderer (Wilson, 1990). In the 1980s, when law enforcement authorities started to differentiate between various kinds of killings, the term "serial killer" became more widely used in the United States popular lexicon and media.

We only see or hear about serial killers in the movies or true-crime novels. In the distant past, serial killers like Jack the Ripper roamed the streets of London, England. Because of this, most Americans believe serial homicides are very rare and can be easily tracked down by law enforcement. As a general rule, serial murderers are those who commit three or more murders overcome time, with at least a month between each murder to satisfy their aberrant psychological needs. When it comes to identifying serial murderers, various agencies use different standards. It is not uncommon for a threshold of three murders to be lowered or increased by the police.

TYPES

- In a serial murder, the perpetrator murders two or more victims in separate occurrences that are unconnected to each other.

- The term "mass murder" refers to an occurrence in which one or more people are killed at the same time and location.

- A spree killer is someone who commits many murders in a shorperiodme, with little time to cool down between attacks.

- Cannibalism is the practice of eating the flesh of another human being.
- The term "cult" is often used to denigrate some sects of Christianity.

Fantasy Of Serial Killer

As soon as a serial killer kills his first victim, he sets in motion a mental process known as a 'cyclical mechanism,' which pushes him to commit other killings. Every time a ritualistic killing takes place, one or more mental pictures are transferred into the actual world, and this process is doomed to repeat. To modify reality, substitute somethinganalyzees previous events, and foresee the future, a person must use his or her imagination to do so. Adults, as well as children, often use this tactic to achieve and keep control over imagined scenarios. Imagine any feeling, such as rage, and it starts to take form with a clear aim in mind and a defined path. Childhood is a time when children may escape into imagination and project what they have learned or experienced as a method of interacting with others, depending on their home situation.

The serial killer's existence revolves around fantasy, and as a result, fantasy plays a significant part in the crimes he commits. The murderer is not only compelled to murder as a result of their mental habits but is also inspired to do so by invasive dream life. Violence towards other people is considered "natural" and "okay" in the minds of those who grew up believing this technique of gaining what they desire. Because of their conflicted feelings about society's standards, they are tempted by this murder case. Many fantasies are reflected in the crime. Many serial murderers' belief systems show indications of unconscious fantasy, even if they had no intention of killing anybody consciously. The serial killer's sexual fantasies are woven into the crime itself. Such aspects as the state of the corpse, how the body is dressed and positioned, and how the disposal location is visible are all evocative of the fantasy in crime scenes. With time, the potential assassin's dependence on fantasies only grows. Instead of feeling in control, it serves as an outlet for frustration and resentment, as well as a way to overcome emotions of inadequacy and failure in general. The potential murderer has acquired a variety of undesirable personality characteristics as a consequence of their dependency on imagination and childhood maltreatment, which only leads to increasing isolation. Autoerotic predilection, violence, chronic lying, rebelliousness, and a penchant for fetish behavior are just a few of these features. The killer's inability to tell the difference between fact and fiction has only become worse over time. The potential killer's social skills are hampered because of his or her bad personality characteristics and inability to tell the difference between dream and reality. The antisocial behavior fuels the isolation, which in turn leads to further isolation. The killer's isolation and antisocial conduct create a feedback loop, culminating in even more violent and isolated behavior on the killer's side. The absence of repercussions for the potential killer's violent actions serves as a kind of reinforcement. " As a result, the killer's childhood fantasies and thought habits only serve to further alienate them from others. Because of early antisocial conduct and imagination, a child's dependence on fantasy intensifies. Anger in society grows as a result of this social exclusion. As a youngster, the murderer relied on imagination and was abused by his parents, which led him to turn to violence. The isolation of a kid rises as a result of the youngster's aggressive behavior as a result of his or her anger. Anger, aggressive behavior, and a licensee on imagination rise as a result of isolation. In the self-feeding cycle of isolation, rage, and fantasy, the prospective murderer is only pushed farther and further away from society's definition of normal. The importance of imagination as a solitary coping mechanism is well-established by the period of sexual development and autoerotic exploration. What has gone wrong here is man's capacity to rehearse and anticipate favorable comes, and to reinforce himself via preparation and planning, as well as through imagination and fantasy. The serial murderer, although thoughts to be steady and secure, is insecure. Being out of control makes the assassin feel weak and powerless.

Fantasy, like other addictions, provides a transient sense of self-worth. A lack of self-worth may explain the excessive brutality perpetrated by certain assassins. poor self-esteem was shown to be associated with violent crime, particularly among those of ordinary or above-average intellect. This is a world where the murderer is always in charge and always strong. It's gotten to the point where the killer's dream has become a reality, one that's just as real as the rest of us. A murderer's fantasy world has become so vivid in his mind that it simply can't discern the two. Murder is not a one-time occurrence as the media and the general public believe. Because it is a natural extension of the serial killer's fantasies, it is reasonable. Murder is propelled by a sense of fantasy. The murder itself has, in a way, cemented a dream that existed before the murder occurred. The inability of the serial murderer to tell the difference between imagination and reality has been exacerbated by the commission of a murder. In the serial killer's mind, the dream has become a reality because of the serial killer's acting out of it. According to the:

"the criminal feels he can now control reality". To paraphrase, "sexual homicide is an act of control, domination, and performance that represents an underlying dream intertwined with violence, sexuality, and death. " It is true that the serial murderer indeed commits to stains the fantasy, even if this is not immediately apparent in all instances. The only way to keep a murderous dream alive is to act it out. The fantasy may have needed to be protected for several reasons, some of which are external, such as the victim interrupting the offender's sense of authority or being angry by the victim's actions. By the killer's admission, he does not recognize the crime. Because of this, the majority of murderers claim to have an "unbearable" drive to murder. The killer's imagination has been elevated as a result of this murder. The respite from acute tension that the serial killer gets from committing the murders is only one of the many advantages that the murders provide for the serial murderer. A compulsion or an addiction, for example, might provide comparable relief. Most serial killings are set off by stress, much as stress may set off binge drinking episodes in alcoholics. Interestingly, after the first or second killing, some assassins become so distraught that they turn themselves into the police. As a general rule, the more murders a serial murderer commits, the more psychological benefit he or she receives. The killer's delusions persist and grow, and his conduct is encouraged. Similar to how fantasy and isolation fueled each other, murder nourishes the fantasy and the fantasy inspires murder. Despite his best efforts, the serial murderer does not come to an end on his own. If the serial murderer is not stopped, he or she will continue to carry out heinous acts of violence. The thrill of a well-executed murder is both reassuring and motivating for the murderer. Quite simply, serial murderers prefer to kill more often to reserve their psychological equilibrium. Because of the imagination and mental euphoria that they experience, they become more aggressive and more willing to take risks. The fantasy becomes stronger with each kg. The murderer is no longer satisfied with murdering once; he has to kill again, and as the number of murders grows, he needs them more often. The kills are the only thing that gives the killer a sense of accomplishment and self-worth. Following this tendency, serial murderers will continue to kill more often. By this point, there are no more internal factors that can stop the serial murderer. Some might say that the serial murderer is an addict rather than some monstrous monster of unfathomable evil. Because of a chaotic background and poor education, the serial murderer develops a coping strategy that is based on imagination. In some ways, this is no different from an alcoholic taking their favorite drink to cope. The serial killer's life starts to revolve around fantasy in the same way as drug addicts do until everything in their existence revolves around the addictive substance. The revolution takes over to the point that the serial killer's existence revolves around fantasies. When it comes to the serial murderer, much like a heroin addict, he is oblivious to the dream that drives him to murder. To summarize, the serial killer's cycle is no different from that of any other addict, with murder serving the same functional aim as heroin theft.

When a youngster experiences hostility or hates in the actual world, the child will develop a personal fantasy world and project that animosity or hatred. A person's self-imagination has no bounds when they are in a state of fantasy. In contrast to a non-criminal, a criminal feels he has the divine right to indulge his desires free of moral or legal constraints Serial murderers' imagination plays a big part in their fantasies about how they might show their power over another human being. The omnipotence of life and death inspires a sense of awe and control. Until a fresh need or emotional requirement causes him to kill again, he may relish his deeds of the murder. As a pawn in a checker's game, the victim of a serial killer is just another piece of the puzzle.

As a way to cope with their social isolation, these people escape into a dream world where their imaginations rule. When it comes to serial killers, fantasies are always the driving force behind their actions, no matter what the motivation for their crimes is.

THOUGHTS AND PATTERNS OF SERIAL KILLERS:

All serial murderers go through a period of distorted thinking. The individual is unable to adequately evaluate the repercussions of deviant conduct because he is more concerned with the emotional fulfillment that may follow from his acts than he is with the long-term ramifications.

When a person moves into this stage of motivation, a single incident or sequence of events, real or imagined, may occur. Disrupted thinking leads the individual to respond excessively to events, making the stimulus seem personal to the person being affected.

It's at this moment that the killer needs to cope with his own emotions of inadequacy as well as the signals he receives from the people around him.

During the external negative reaction phase, the subject's superiority as a person is reinforced. When he commits crimes, he has no regard for the repercussions.

The subject is returned to a state of equilibrium at the beginning of this phase. The assassin also considers ways to reduce the dangers to himself or herself in impending killings.

BIOLOGICAL POSITIONS OF A SERIAL KILLER:

Serial murderers' unimaginable and heinous acts typically elicit the skepticism of the general public. The beginnings of a serial murderer are critical to understanding. These questions may be answered using the three-phase model that was created.

Some people have a genetic propensity to violence owing to brain system abnormalities, including a low threshold for irritation. Stress and environmental trauma are two additional factors that contribute to the erratic structure of the brain. All that's left of the actual world is the criminal behavior that the serial killer had previously dreamt about and that has led him to conduct his first murder.

Other than confronting reality, he chooses to withdraw into a fantasy world that satisfies him. A time of relative peace follows the murder, during which he elaborates and relieves the murder he just did in his dream, until, once again, imagining is not enough and he will need to kill again.

> ➢ The stage of skewed thinking is one that all serial murderers go through. Since the shift to this stage, it is impossible for a subject to fully analyze the effect of a deviant act;
>
> ➢ motivating phase: an event or group of events, which are actual or imagined, because the subject is more interested in the emotional satisfaction that may arise from his activities. To compensate for the subject's skewed thinking, the stimulus is experienced as something personal. A physical

release is required, and that is what happens when the subject starts seeking prey/victim.

➢ The internal negative response phase: the killer must now cope with emotions of inadequacy, particularly when negative signals from society are present. His fragile sense of self-identity necessitates a strong feeling of dominance, control, and violence, which he uses to achieve so.

➢ The individual receives confirmation of his superiority by an external unfavorable reaction. The prospective repercussions of his illicit deeds don't pique his curiosity in the least. Increase and stabilize one's feeling of authority by engaging in this conduct

➢ The fifth phase is called "restoration," and it aims to bring the patient back to equilibrium. Now that the serial murderer has returned to this frame of mind, he considers previously overlooked harmful repercussions and realizes that his method has to be enhanced by correctly picking the victims and dealing with where to put the corpses so that they may be readily located." Additionally, the murderer ponders how to reduce his or her dangers in future killings. By returning to "distorted thinking," the individual completes the cycle.

➤ Childhood of a serial killer:

Some serial murderers are not victims of childhood abuse; some serial killers are not victims of childhood abuse. A link between them cannot be ignored as a mere coincidence. Behavioral decisions might be affected by personal tragedies

As an example, persons with a certain version of the enzyme monoamine-oxidase-A gene are more likely to engage in aggressive conduct if they were raised in an abusive household. There is no guarantee that a youngster who is genetically predisposed to aggressive behavior will become a criminal. The combination of heredity and environment, such as traumatic childhood events, is what shapes a person's personality.

TRIGGER:

A trigger is a brief event in a serial killer's life that sets off the killer's instincts and propels him or her into the first murder. In rare cases, a serial killer might go on a self-imposed exile from the practice if he does not locate the perfect trigger.

When a person commits at least one felony killing before moving on to the next, we call that person a serial killer. A serial killer kills several people over an extended period to satisfy his or her own psychological needs. A serial murderer, according to certain authorities and psychiatrists, must commit at least three murders before being labeled as one. In addition, serial killings are carried out to demonstrate one's authority over the victim. Childhood experiences have a profound effect on serial killers and mass murderers alike. In the meanwhile, their social withdrawal and violent nature are fueled by their carelessness. In addition to his motives, a serial killer's successive killings are carried out by the serial killer on his or her own without the supervision of a political, governmental, criminal, or intelligence entity. This is a crucial characteristic of a serial murderer.

Because of their very nature, serial murderers are wicked. Irrational conduct is characteristic of serial murderers, which is why they commit homicide so often. They become recidivists and murder innocent people because of their bad motives. Psychologists have shown that murdering people is quite pleasurable for the vast majority of serial murderers. They are distinct from one-time killers in that they derive greater joy from murdering again because of the psychological fulfillment they obtain from killing others. These convicted felons have a deep-seated desire to kill for their benefit.

Some serial murderers believe they have a responsibility to rid the world of undesirables, such as prostitutes, homosexuals, drug dealers, or persons from a different race or religion.

These are known as "mission-oriented" serial killers. In general, they are not psychotic, and they believe their murders benefit society and the world as a whole. To track down the mission-oriented murderers, the crime scene must be controlled by the kind of person they are targeting.

OPERATIONAL STYLE OF SERIAL KILLERS

The most prevalent approach used by serial killers to commit murder is called Modus Operandi. The offender's method of action is known as the Modus Operandi. As an example, tying up his victims at the murder site is a necessary tool for the killer. The Modus Operandi, in other words, is a learned behavior that may be altered.

The murdering of a female relative for the sake of family honor is the most common kind of honor killing is claimed by a family member or close friend of the rapist that the victim has tarnished the family's reputation or name.

It is common in a patriarchal society to keep tabs on the actions of women and minors. First, her father and brothers, then her spouse, are held responsible for ensuring that a woman's "sexual purity" is maintained. "Sexually immoral" activities, such as publicly chatting with men who are not related to one's husband, are often cited as reasons for honor killing victims' deaths (even if they are the victims of rape or sexual assault). If she refuses to join an arranged marriage or divorce or separates from her violent spouse, she may be targeted by assassins for any number of different reasons. Men's sentiments and impressions, rather than facts, sometimes drive an assault on a woman simply because she is suspected of doing anything that might harm the reputation of her family. Female relatives, however, are more likely to support the atrocities and even participate in their perpetuation.

Changes in circumstances or new abilities and knowledge may necessitate changes in a serial killer's method of operation. For example, the criminal may discover that bringing handcuffs to the site of the crime is both simpler and more effective than tying up the victim with rope. When Jack the Ripper attacked prostitutes on the street at night with a knife, this was his method of operation.

It is possible to create a profile of a typical serial killer by gathering the behavioral and developmental features. saying that the serial murderer is a unique and exceptionally dangerous criminal He has a superficial charm that allows him to simulate proper socially acceptable conduct in any situation.

The majority of serial murderers grew up in abusive, dysfunctional, and neglectful families. According to the findings, serial killers often have a history of substance misuse in their families. There was a parent with drug addiction, crime, and deviant sexual conduct present in the household of the murders, according to the evaluation. A lack of self-worth was a constant thread in the childhoods of all killers. While there is a correlation between criminal behavior and a person's personality, psychology, and upbringing,

Children who were abused as children were more likely to become serial murderers, a pioneering study of 50 serial killers showed. A considerably larger proportion than the general population of serial murderers, according to the study's author, were mistreated as children. Perhaps the kind of abuse they were subjected to as a child has an impact on a serial killer's behavior and choice of victims.

There's no way around the truth that most individuals who experience abuse don't go on to become serial murderers. One-third of the serial murderers included in this study had no prior history of abuse, the researchers found.

Parents who physically and verbally abuse their children create in their offspring an almost intrinsic need for violence as a first reaction to any problems. Understanding how childhood trauma and sexual aggression impact victims of serial killers was explored

Before killing their victims, serial murderers who had been abused as children were more likely to sexually attack them. In contrast, serial murderers who were not abused as children did not engage in sexually violent conduct (Serial Killers: relation between childhood maltreatment and sexual relations with the victim)

FEMALE SERIAL KILLER

Women who commit serial murders may be classified in several ways. Labels such as "Black Widow" and "Angel Of Death" were used to designate the murderers. They also called them "Team Killers" and "Unsolved" about their motives. Most women were classified as either black widows or team murderers when categorized in this manner, according to the research team.

Female serial murderers might be driven by a variety of motives, including attention-seeking, drug addiction, or other psychopathological traits. In popular culture, a "black widow" refers to a female serial killer who kills males to make money. These killers are typically emotionally attached to their victims, and this emotional connection is often required to commit a crime.

In most cases, female serial killers use low-tech methods such as poisoning their victims to hide their murders (the preferred choice for killing)

Suffocation (16 percent), stabbing (11 percent), and drowning (10 percent) are some methods used by female serial killers (5 percent). They may choose to attack a single area, such as their own home or a medical facility, or a large number of targets in a single city or state at once. While most female serial killers do their crimes in the comfort of their own homes, there is one notable exception: a killer who committed her crimes outside of the house, with a handgun rather than poison, and who targeted strangers rather than family or friends.

JUVENILE

Young serial murderers are quite uncommon. Juvenile serial murderers may be classified in three ways: primary, mature, or secondary killers, depending on their stage of development. Comparing and contrasting these three groups has been the subject of research, which has shown some interesting parallels and contrasts between them learn more about adult serial murderers by studying those who commit the crimes while they are still in their teens or early twenties. A young serial killer is in reality, the youngest death row inmate.

THRILL

For the thrill-seekers, the main goal is to inflict pain or fright on their victims to get a rush of adrenaline. Hunters and killers alike want the rush of adrenaline that comes with stalking and murdering prey. Thrill murderers are simply interested in getting the thrill of the kill, and their attacks are seldom extended or sexual. For the most part, the victims are strangers, albeit the murderer may have been following them for some time. It is possible to refrain from murdering for lengthy periods while yet becoming a successful thrill killer. It is a common misconception that the ideal crime would go undetected.

MOTIVES

Four types of motivations are often used to categorize serial killers: the hedonistic need for pleasure and self-fulfillment; nonetheless, the motivations of any particular murderer may show substantial overlap among these categories. The World of Serial Murderers has categorized serial killers into four distinct groups. In the first case, a serial murderer is described as a "visionary." Voices or visions instruct the visionary serial killer to murder.

The second sort of serial murderer is known as a "mission serial killer." It is the goal of the mission of serial killers to purge the community of undesirables. This is the third category of a serial murderer. The hedonistic serial killer is driven by a need for gratification in the form of thrills, pleasure, and ease. Last but not least, we have the power/control of serial murderers. Motivation for the power/control serial killer is a desire for control and dominance.

ANALYSIS

In addition to homicidal tendencies, serial killers are more prone to participate in and display varying degrees of mental illness or psychopathy. Criminals who commit serial murder fall into one of three groups, according to the FBI's crime classification handbook. These individuals are classified as either "organized" or "non-organized" serial murderers. In many cases, they entice the victims using ruses that appeal to their feeling of altruism They are swift and effective at killing their victims, and they possess social and other interpersonal abilities that allow them to form close friendships and sexual relationships with other people. They are also unlikely to harm anybody in the process. Unplanned, impulsive, and less likely to conceal their victims' bodies are the hallmarks of serial murderers with a criminal record.

They are most likely to be jobless, a loner, or both, with few acquaintances, and they may have a history of mental illness and extreme violence on their record. Forensic and remedial professionals have a huge task in establishing the link between the serial murderer, the crime, and the likely reason or purpose for such horrible murders. The motives and compulsions of serial murderers are unknown. The solution to the crime against society may lie in a multidisciplinary approach. According to Sears, these people's dissatisfaction might be exacerbated by their social exclusion.

This buildup of energy originating from the existence of an insufficient homelike that caused an incapacity to deal with failure results in an outburst of aggressive conduct. In his research, Sears discovered that serial murderers are more likely to lack a caring and supportive connection with their parents. Violence is more likely to be shown in adults who were mistreated as children, according to research. In addition, he discovered that moms and serial murderers had a strange connection.

SYNDROME HAVING A SERIAL KILLER

In addition to homicidal tendencies, serial killers are more prone to participate in and display varied degrees of mental illness or psychopath. Criminals who commit serial murder fall into one of three groups, according to the FBI's crime classification handbook. These individuals are classified as either "organized" or "non-organized" serial murderers. In many cases, they entice the victims using ruses that appeal to their feeling of altruism They are swift and effective at killing their victims, and they possess social and other interpersonal abilities that allow them to form close friendships and sexual relationships with other people. They are also unlikely to harm anybody in the process. Unplanned, impulsive, and less likely to conceal their victims' bodies are the hallmarks of serial murderers with a criminal record.

They are most likely to be jobless, a loner, or both, with few acquaintances, and they may have a history of mental illness and extreme violence on their record.

Forensic and remedial professionals have a huge task in establishing the link between the serial murderer, the crime, and the likely reason or purpose for such horrible murders. The motives and compulsions of serial murderers are unknown. The solution to the crime against society may lie in a multidisciplinary approach. According to Sears, these people's dissatisfaction might be exacerbated by their social exclusion.

This buildup of energy originating from the existence of an insufficient homelike that caused an incapacity to deal with failure results in an outburst of aggressive conduct. In his research, Sears discovered that serial murderers are more likely to lack a caring and supportive connection with their parents. Violence is more likely to be shown in adults who were mistreated as children, according to research. In addition, he discovered that moms and serial murderers had a strange connection.

Most serial murderers grew up in homes where they were exposed to 21 patterns or symptoms of episodic violent behavior, which serve as a profile or propensity for future serial killers. Ritualistic behavior, insanity masks, compulsivity, seeking help, severe memory impairments and a chronic inability to tell the truth, suicidal tendencies, histories of serious assault, abnormal sexual behavior and hypersexuality, birth injuries, chronic drug and alcohol use, and extraordinary cruelty toward criminals are all examples of aggressive behavior patterns.

This list is a great explanation of what it's like to be a serial killer. Some individuals can better manage their drives to kill than others, according to Strean and Freeman in their book Our Wish To Kill. If you're furious with your husband, partner, or children and spout out a remark like that, I'm going to be so enraged I'm ready to murder you. That person could you truly kill.

That question is unanswered in the academic literature. Psychiatrists have never been able to explain murder, particularly serial murder. Although there are many similar traits among serial killers, no one has been able to crack their criminal minds. narcissistic, uncaring, and unhealthy families.

CHARACTER ANALYSIS OF SERIAL KILLERS:

The serial murderer has undergone a dramatic shift since its debut. Rather than horrible entities out to wreak devastation only for the sake of it, they are now seen as three-dimensional people having motivations for their actions. Research on serial murderers has also allowed us to identify patterns that may be used to create fictional serial killers with distinct personalities and clichés. As a result, stereotypes and tropes based on their numerous similar characteristics have been developed. There are many sub-types of serial murderers, as well as physical and personal characteristics that make up the contemporary serial killer cliché.

Murderers' diseased brains transform pain and death into a burning need to kill. Serial murderers, in contrast to "normal" people, are driven by a desire for gory delights and an addiction to murder. Because of the way serial murderers are depicted on television, most people think they are evil. If we take the attractive serial murderer Dexter as an example, although he does lead a regular life, he takes it upon himself to eliminate all of the "bad men" in the world to fulfill his need to kill. Then there's Freddy Krueger, who murders people in their nightmares and causes their deaths in the real world as well. Hannibal Lecter is another notorious serial murderer, It's not only in movies and television that these fictitious serial murderers inspire terror; in real life, people are afraid of them as well. Several of these films and television programs attempt to convince us that these fictitious murderers and settings are real. There is no way to determine a serial murderer by their looks, contrary to popular opinion and fictitious movies. What is it like to be a real-life serial killer? Conscious patterns of conduct identify a real-life serial murderer from the rest of the criminal population. By their purposeless and senseless antisocial conduct, lack of conscience, and emotional vacuum, serial killers/psychopaths are identified. They're risk-takers who have no fear." Similarly, murder is either a natural decision or a choice driven by a passion for all serial murderers. However, the sorts of serial murderers and their degrees of expertise are vastly different.

To begin, serial murderers may be classified according to one of four motivational types. Visionary, mission-oriented, hedonistic, and power/control are the four subtypes. Other subcategories exist, and a person may have motives that cross over into many different groupings even though there are four main types. Delusions and hallucinations might inspire a visionary murderer to carry out the crime. Often, they think they're better than others.

BEHAVIORAL ANALYSIS OF SERIAL KILLERS:

Some murder investigations don't provide enough evidence to warrant an arrest at the beginning of the inquiry. For example, a murderer's manner may be used to limit the kind of person who committed the crime. According to the FBI's Behavioral Analysis Unit, it may be difficult for local and state authorities to determine a killer's psychological and behavioral characteristics. At first, it was called "criminal profiling," but the FBI's BAU team of experts has renamed it "behavioral analysis.". When it comes to criminal profiling, behavioral analysts (also known as criminal profilers) can infer a person's personality based on their activities during the crime itself, according to behavioral analysis.

Alcohol and drug addiction, a lonely and solitary childhood, dreams of harming and murdering people, and playing out fantasies about animals all contributed to the development of a violent personality. Before attacking people, they often target defenseless animals.

Accidental or repetitive brain trauma, as well as injuries sustained at birth, have been linked to aggressive and violent behavior. The limbic, hypothalamic, or temporal lobe regions of the brain may be involved in episodes of spontaneous aggressiveness. Seizures and other types of amnesia may arise from lesions to these parts of the brain, which are associated with hormones, aggressiveness, emotion, and motivation.

At least 70% of serial murderers had severe brain injuries as children or teenagers, demonstrating the connection between severe head traumas and serial killing. The pre-frontal cortex (the part of the brain that deals with planning and decision-making) may not operate correctly in psychopaths, according to some studies.

Someone can have all of the characteristics of a serial murderer and yet not be a serial killer. No matter how similar we are, we will never harm another living thing or human being.

They have a strong desire to murder others, and they go out of their way to achieve that goal. Granted, the need to murder someone may not be a conscious decision; rather, it may be a compulsion resulting from a mental illness.

The characteristics of serial murderers might be very different from one another. I'd have to presume that they don't feel the same way about murdering that the majority of people do, but this lack of feeling might be due to a variety of factors.

Behavioral analysis has been employed by several law enforcement agencies to determine the most probable features of the perpetrator of a given crime or series of crimes. During and after a crime, an offender may demonstrate behavioral and personality traits that they are unaware of. The "why" and "how" of a crime may be gleaned from a crime scene's verbal and nonverbal cues and behavior's via the use of behavioral analysis. Even though behavioral analysis may be used for a wide range of crimes.

CRIME SCENE MASKING:

Staging and masking are the two main approaches to crime scene preparation. It is common for murderers to stage their victims in ways that are psychologically soothing, degrading to the victim, or designed to convey a certain message to the police. When a criminal tries to cover up the truth by altering a crime scene, it is called staging. An example of this would be when a murderer sets fire to the site of the crime to fool investigators into thinking the victim perished in an accident.

The term "crime scene masking" refers to the cleaning and removal of evidence and/or the corpse from the site of a murder. Masking is used to obfuscate evidence, evade law enforcement, and escape being convicted of a crime by obfuscating the evidence. Male criminals are much more likely to stage and disguise their crimes than females, according to the statistics.

Masking, on the other hand, comes with some major risks. If a murderer lingers at a crime scene for lengthy periods and touches, moves, or cleans up a lot of things, they will leave behind more evidence. Crime scene masking increases evidence of the murderer, not decreases it.

In addition, the longer it takes to disguise, the more likely it is that a family member, neighbor, or bystander may catch the perpetrator at the scene.

when the crime is taking place the second or disguised, police must immediately seek anybody who has a known link to the victim or the crime site. This is because only assassins who have a strong emotional attachment to the crime site or victim are more inclined to clean up after themselves after doing the deed. To clean up the murder scene, even if a killer has no connection to the location or victim, he or she is unlikely to stay since the extra effort is not worthwhile.

The former Chief of Police, a 24-year veteran of law enforcement, was contacted because of his extensive knowledge of murder investigations. A clean-up had been conducted or attempted at several murder locations he had gone to. Every one of the killings was perpetrated by someone close to the victim who was either a known acquaintance or an old buddy of the killer.

SIGNIFICANCE OF MOVEMENT OF SERIAL KILLER'S BODY:

Even more dangerous than disguising is moving the corpse of a deceased victim from the principal crime scene to a secondary location. Killers often transport their victims from one crime site to another by loading them into a vehicle and driving them to a different area where they may be unloaded.

The longer it takes to dig a hand-dug grave to effectively bury the corpse at a separate location, the greater the likelihood that the perpetrator will be apprehended by the police.

The more time the murderer spends with the victim's corpse, the more likely it is that a passerby will find them. Only if the murderer believes they would be the most likely suspect if the corpse is found at the major crime scene will they take the great risk of moving the body

first brought up the issue of criminals relocating bodies, made an interesting point regarding the psychology involved during our conversation. Individuals are often reluctant to get into touch with a bleeding or dead body on purpose, according to their assessment of the situation. It's a complicated position both physically and psychologically. To even touch a body, much less dismember it, wrap it, carry it, drive it to a secondary place, and dump it, requires a lot of mental strength and self-control (e.g., not vomiting). A lot of people can't handle this at this point.

When a victim's corpse has been moved, the police investigating the crime site should initially seek anybody else who has a direct link to the crime scene. After a person's death, it is nearly often done by a family member or a best friend decrease with wishes here's a strong possibility this person is responsible.

DETERMINATION OF SERIAL KILLER MOTIVES:

As long as proof of a killer's motive is available, it is very beneficial for prosecutors when pursuing criminal charges against them. Disguising conduct and the removal of the body from the site of the crime need to determine the murderer's motive and the goal of the post-offense cleaning and removal. Anger/emotion, greed/attention-seeking, and mental illness/psychological need are the most prevalent causes of murder.

Classic serial murder is different from spree serial murder, which is more likely to be driven by a need for thrill-seeking than sexual fulfillment. Like political assassinations, terrorist attacks, or gangster-class murder, most serial murders are not carried out for financial gain. Many people feel that sexual urges or simply the desire to have a fun drive serial murderers. To give the murderers influence over their victims, which may or may not be sexual, many murders are committed.

Migrant women, prostitutes, minors, homosexuals, and other squatters are among the most often targeted demographics in these attacks. Serial murderers have received a lot of media attention because they are perceived as personifications of evil.

To avoid humiliation or disgrace, the most prevalent reasons for concealing or relocating a body are self-preservation and self-interest. Killers who clean up the scene of a crime are said to be motivated by self-preservation to divert police attention and evade suspicion. Suicides and other unintentional deaths are more likely to have a purpose of shame or humiliation than murders. Loved ones try to improve a problematic circumstance to lessen the victim's perceived shame when they witness the victim in distress.

SOCIETY ANALYSIS OF THE STRANGER

As a result of the unparalleled degree of anonymity brought about by contemporary urbanization, mass urbanization has become a defining feature of our day. When people lived in premier communities, they knew one another by name and were familiar with their neighbors' family histories, daily schedules, hobbies, and other personal preferences. As a result, the presence of strangers was a topic of gossip and suspicion. In medieval times, the typical person could have only encountered 100 strangers in their lifetime, a very low amount when compared to today, when a person may encounter hundreds of strangers only on the daily commute to work.

It was the growth of capitalism and widespread migration to cities that resulted in people being surrounded by strangers. Serial killers, who are notorious for preying on strangers, have become more common in recent years, which has contributed to the emergence of this trend they don't include any previous connection between the perpetrator and the victim, unlike other killings in which a link between the killer and the victim is required. Serial killings are well-suited to the routine, impersonal interactions prevalent in densely populated modern metropolises.

Society indeed has a significant impact on our lives, whether favorable or harmful. it is the reality that the term "society." Nearly every one of these serial murderers has suffered from mental abuse at some point in their lives, whether it was inflicted by society or members of their own families. As they mature, they begin to retaliate against people they perceive to be responsible for making them feel so despised and worthless. A person who has been treated nicely throughout their life is unlikely to embark on a murdering spree for no apparent cause. Some may argue that even the happiest individuals can be serial murderers, but I don't believe it. They're incorrect. Abuse may begin as early as infancy in certain cases. People were never meant to endure the daily torment of being harassed for their looks or mental states, particularly on an ongoing basis. I place the guilt squarely on the shoulders of society, their siblings, and their parents for failing to do anything to stop the sibling bullying. Those school shootings don't bother you. When a gunman picks out a specific victim, the rest of society takes the side of the victim, feeling sorry for the deceased and enraged at the shooter. These same kids tormented the shooter daily, and the school's values are unable to stop them. In most circumstances, I don't hold the shooter responsible. Society may be cruel. In school, bullying and ganging up on someone is acceptable because the popular students, who everyone admires and wants to be friends with, are considered the cool clique. However, if the person being tormented has no friends to support them, the bullying will go unchecked. he or she will be ostracized. They have the potential to be both gorgeous and caring. Although they may be nice and caring toward others, if someone has even the slightest physical flaw, such as a large nose, stuttering difficulties, facial deformities, or just being intellectually challenged, they will be instantly marginalized. I believe that society is to blame for the rise of serial murderers. For the victims of serial murderers, I am sorry. Most of the time, they haven't done anything wrong. When society strips away a person's self-respect and self-worth, it may have a detrimental influence on his or her well-being.

There are many distinct sorts of serial murderers, and the underlying causes of their crimes remain unknown. Almost all of them are certainly psychopaths, and no one understands what causes them.

Psychopaths and sociopaths often lead completely regular lives, and in some cases, they even thrive in their chosen professions. They may become prolific and sophisticated murderers if they suffer from a drive to kill. It's been years since I've been noticed. There are many instances to choose from. Once again, no one has a clue as to why certain individuals are born emotionally devoid, and no one ever will.

It is neither political, domestic, nor for-profit that serial murderers commit their crimes. Serial murderers kill for the sake of killing, and they do it again and over again. An expert on serial killings in South Africa has defined the killers as people with damaged souls who have an "inborn desire, driven by imagination, which may lead to torture, and/or sexual abuse and mutilation and necrophilia" in their motivation Psychosis, paranoia, schizophrenia, and other mental illnesses are all common among serial murderers. Others have been labeled as psychopaths. However, the body's remedies aren't sufficient. There must have been a significant incident or person in a person's upbringing that sparked these feelings of rage and aggression. Nature and nurture both have a part in the development of a serial murderer.

Killers aren't all mistreated children. Not every murderer was scarred for life by a traumatic occurrence. A small percentage of serial killers seem to spontaneously transform into homicidal monsters. They grew reared in normal, healthy households and showed no signs of being serial killers. There are three notorious serial murderers in the nature category: Ted Bundy, Donald Harvey, and Denis Radar. Even though none of the three was ever abused or neglected, the country was shocked by their conduct.

Conclusion

The state of Al Society is precarious due to a grave crisis that is wreaking havoc on its members. Everywhere in the globe, some serial murderers target anybody who stands in their path. Detecting a murderer if you don't comprehend the person's thinking and mentality is almost difficult. The knowledge of serial killers is significant since it is crucial to be cautious with everyone. People need to be aware of them to protect themselves and their loved ones. There is a need for people to assess all of the information they have about both the perpetrator and the victim. To create the profiles, we need to understand the different sorts of serial murderers and the various mental illnesses they may be suffering from.

Serial murderers who are part of a larger organization pose the greatest threat However, they seem to be like everyone else, but they have a serious issue. With an average IQ of between 105 and 120, most serial murderers fall under this category. To acquire the confidence of the serial murderers, they are very friendly. Many intricacies go into planning a crime, so they don't leave any evidence to implicate them. They use seduction to infiltrate the crime scene and take control of it. They won't have any issues talking to the cops. Disorganized murderers, on the other hand, have an average IQ of between 80 and 95. It is difficult for them to make friends, and they often live on their own. They also tend to be unstable individuals. For the most part, they don't plot their crimes. They're more evident than the gangs that commit mass murders regularly.

An antisocial personality disorder is characterized by an inability to distinguish right from wrong. Nobody mattered to them; all they cared about was getting what they wanted. they show no rumors and can discuss their misdeeds openly without repercussion. In the second condition, known as multiple personality disorder, a person has an altered personality that influences their actions. It is said that the alters arise spontaneously and unintentionally, and they operate independently of one other. The difficulty is that each of these alters personalities make their own decisions, and since the others are unaware of what their alter egos are doing, they may murder. Bipolar disorder, the last but not least, is characterized by extreme ups and downs in mood, energy, perspective, and conduct. This ranges from the euphoric peaks of manic behavior to the depressive lows of depression. And unlike normal mood swings, bipolar disorder's mood shifts are so severe that they hurt their capacity to perform. They are prone to mood swings, which might cause them to get enraged and murder.

www.ingramcontent.com/pod-product-compliance
Lightning Source LLC
Chambersburg PA
CBHW061644250726
48659CB00004B/1371